SAFARI PRESS
T0303096

The Hunting Instinct

The Hunting Instinct

Safari Chronicles on Hunting, Game Conservation, and Management in the Republic of South Africa and Namibia: 1990–1998

by

Philip D. Rowter

Safari Press Inc.

P. O. Box 3095, Long Beach, CA 90803

Rowter, Philip D.

Second edition

Safari Press Inc.

1999, Long Beach, California

ISBN 1-57157-158-2

Library of Congress Catalog Card Number: 98-75349

10 9 8 7 6 5 4 3 2

Readers wishing to receive the Safari Press catalog, featuring many fine books on big-game hunting, wingshooting, and sporting firearms, should write to Safari Press Inc., P.O. Box 3095, Long Beach, CA 90803, USA. Tel: (714) 894-9080 or visit our Web site at www.safaripress.com.

Table of Contents

Acknowledgments vii
Introduction viii
About the Author: Who is Philip D. Rowter, anyway? xi

Chapter 1 Cape Buffalo 1
Chapter 2 Leopard 9
Chapter 3 Elephant 25
Chapter 4 Lion 37
Chapter 5 Southern White Rhinoceros 47
Chapter 6 Hippopotamus 55
Chapter 7 Hunting Plains Game 83
- Bushbuck 84
- Greater Kudu 89
- Oryx 94
- Impala 97
- Baboon 99
- Red Hartebeest 101
- Blue Wildebeest 105
- Black Wildebeest 108
- Giraffe 111
- Gray or Common Duiker 115
- Bushpig 117
- Klipspringer 122
- Spotted Hyena 125
- Warthog 130
- Southern Mountain Reedbuck 134

	Springbok	137
	Waterbuck	139
	Eland	142
	Steenbok	145
	Zebra	148
Chapter 8	Birds: Guinea Fowl and Sandgrouse	157
Chapter 9	Snake Trilogy: Black Mamba	163
Chapter 10	Snake Trilogy: Spitting Cobra	173
Chapter 11	Snake Trilogy: Twig Snake	195
Chapter 12	Dangerous Things and an Underrated Bird	199
Chapter 13	Ticks and Fever	203
Chapter 14	Mosquitoes, Malaria, and Other Torments	207
Chapter 15	Of Honey Badgers and Men	213
Chapter 16	Rogues	221
Chapter 17	Other Dangers of Hunting	227
Chapter 18	Hunt's End	233

Acknowledgments

I would like to acknowledge the initial help I received from Brian Marsh of Zimbabwe and the further help and support given to me by my wife, Judith, and my publisher at Safari Press, Ludo Wurfbain. Others deserving mention are the various PHs, trackers, and skinners without whose help this book would not have been possible.

Introduction

This is a collection of some of my hunting memorabilia. I have also included something about weapons and ammunition, shot placement, ballistics, safety, game management, and tales about encounters with people, animals, reptiles, birds, and insects during several hunting expeditions to Namibia and the Republic of South Africa (RSA). The stories are a record of my experiences. It all happened; maybe serendipity also had something to do with it.

Standard books about hunting tell how the animal was hunted and how it finished up; sometimes there is even a photo to prove it. It's not always like that. Most of the time you draw a blank, despite doing it all the right way. Sometimes you need even more than luck. If you read this book with the anticipation that the hunter always wins, you'll be disappointed—well at least partially. Many of the animals I hunted did get away, and the best of luck to them as well. Hunting, you see, is about two things. It is about what might happen, and it is about attitudes. The first is not under your control. The second definitely is. Hunting is about patience, expertise, humour, sadness, love, hate, caring, and luck. There is no other human activity, except, perhaps, the oldest of them all, that is constructed from such emotional building bricks.

Hunting wild animals is dangerous, and, although the species hunted and the weapons used by man have changed over the millennia, the element of danger has not. We see from the cave paintings of our ancestors that they had to come into close contact with their quarry before they could hurl stones or penetrate its hide with sharpened sticks. The invention of the bow and arrow made it possible to inflict the necessary mortal wounds from much greater distances. Later, with the discovery of chemical propellants (gunpowder, cordite, and nitrocellulose), it became possible for the hunter to fire a bullet or a shower of lead pellets at the quarry with some precision from a considerable distance.

The invention of gunpowder revolutionized hunting and made it unnecessary for the hunter to expose himself to the dangers inherent in close-contact hunting. However, there are still dangers involved, dangers that vary with the species hunted, where and how it is hunted, what weapon and bullet or shot is used, and how near the hunter gets to the quarry. You can die if a small antelope places a horn into your liver. You can also die if an elephant gets you on the floor and then insists that you look at the pattern on the sole of its foot. There is no relationship between the size of an animal and the degree of danger it presents. Even a bee sting can kill you.

Most books on hunting attempt to justify it; this one is no exception. My intention is to give other, less familiar perspectives on hunting, perspectives that have been forgotten as our modern world has become isolated from the real one. The pro and contra arguments surrounding hunting are numerous and have been dealt with elsewhere. For that reason I'll make only a few remarks. As the change to the next millennium approaches, hunting and field sports are drawing increasing hostility. Why? The reasons are many and cover the whole political and social spectrum.

I believe the answer lies in two places. First, modern mankind has become a pantywaist, shielded from the reality of where meat comes from. As long as it is on the butcher's slab with a price ticket on it, it's all right. Second, the burgeoning human population (over six billion by the year 2000, compared with about one billion in 1900) has eroded the habitats of animals. Loss of habitat destroys species more efficiently than hunting ever could, but people still tend to blame hunting. What then can controlled hunting, even in reduced habitats, contribute to the well-being of any species?

Answer: The taking of an old, biologically exhausted (nonbreeding) animal will not directly affect the viable population of a species. If not directly, then, can it indirectly? Answer: The sportsman's trophy fee will be used for game management, which ensures funding for research as well as for securing new land and additional financing for antipoaching units. Like everything else, if it (in this case, the game) pays, it stays. If it stays, use it or lose it. It's as simple as that. No farmer keeps animals (or, come to think about it, crops) that do not pay. Is it unreasonable to expect anything other from governments and game farmers? Remember, the world is not a benevolent fund. It never has been, in any case.

A word about the format used in this book. At the start of each chapter I have, where appropriate, given a few biological facts about the animal concerned. I've also used some writer's license, based on the facts, to involve the reader in previous events leading to the decision to hunt or cull the animal in question. As far as the hunt is concerned, I've simply told it as it happened.

About The Author

I was born in the village of Studley, in Warwickshire, England, on 22 September 1947. The fact that this village is not too far from Stratford-on-Avon has had absolutely no bearing on my literary skills (or weaknesses), although I do happen to like Shakespeare very much! More contemporary writers such as Ruark, Hemingway, and Capstick have contributed to my taste for reading and writing about hunting. My grandfather (who, incidentally, was a poacher of rabbits and pheasants) is also responsible for what lies between these book covers. You see, like you, I can't change my genes, either.

The first thing in my life that I can remember is catching a pigeon with my bare hands; that's a feat of memory, since it happened some years ago. It was also a feat of hunting for a whippersnapper barely out of diapers. The bird, a variety called a tumbler, had been so busy picking up wheat from our loft and had got its head into the upturned bucket that it didn't see me creeping up behind it. Clutching the weakly fluttering bird tightly to my chest I ran to my grandfather to show him my prize. After being severely admonished (it just happened to be grandpappy's prize bird), he forced me, to my utter dismay, to release it. No matter, I had hunted successfully and from that day onward it was clear to me, if not my family, that I was a hunter and would remain so.

Time passed and despite annoying small details like school and education, I still remained true to my chosen profession. Life being what it is, however, you are born for the human race, and then you are consequently and brutally moulded into something for society, which means that you rarely can do what you really want to do. An apprenticeship as a metallurgist was entered into and, to the surprise of all, myself included, successfully completed. Immense pressure now came on me to abandon all and go to university. Yielding to the promise of untold wealth after obtaining a higher degree, I went to Aston University, in Birmingham, England, and did my duty. Leaving a few years later, with my still hot-from-the-press Ph.D. certificate tightly tucked under my arm, I faced the reality of the job-finding jungle, so I promptly left England to Margaret Thatcher and went to make my fortune elsewhere.

My travels took me to Switzerland, then Holland, and back again to the land of the Alps where I still live today. Somewhere along the way I'd also found a Dutch girl who could tolerate me, and I married her. No, it was *not* a shotgun marriage! I learnt the German language and took my hunter's examination for the Canton of Aargau, in northern Switzerland, and passed. I am currently the only Englishman to possess a valid Swiss hunting license.

A year later, much to the dismay of the French, and after having crucified their language, I successfully took the French state hunter's examination. I believe that I am the only Englishman to possess a valid French hunting license as well. Now, after having revenged the defeat of the English by the Normans at Hastings, in 1066, I relaxed my vendetta somewhat against the French as a nation and started hunting there, as well, since I was now armed with theoretical knowledge about the birds, bees, assorted mammals, rifles, bullets, ballistics, and woodcrafts.

The chronicles in this book are a record of some of my hunting experiences in South Africa and Namibia. They are not meant to be the usual sort of hunting, shooting, and fishing stories, but are an attempt to put hunting into another perspective. I hope that I have been successful; if so, you will also see why the hunting instinct endures.

Dedication

In the jungle, the mighty jungle, the lion sleeps tonight . . .
(Words from "The Lion Sleeps Tonight" by Weiss, Peretti, and Creatore)

Don't believe a word of it!
(My comment)

Dedicated to the memory of Peter Hathaway Capstick.
He was a lion among writers and a good hunter.

Chapter 1

Cape Buffalo

(*Syncerus caffer caffer*)

The very words Cape buffalo should be enough to quicken the pulse of anyone who has had anything to do with these animals. If you haven't had the pleasure of meeting this mountain of muscle, gristle, and horn on his own terms in the bush, a photograph will usually suffice to start your adrenaline flowing. These big, black bovines of Beelzebub demand respect. One subspecies of buffalo worth mentioning is the short-tempered red buffalo. It lives in the equatorial forests of Africa, where it searches for food to eat and people to kill (just for fun), apparently with equal avidity. We will not bother here with *Syncerus caffer nana,* the dwarf red forest buffalo. We have already more than enough on our hands with its big cousin, the Cape buffalo. The beasts have equally delightful table manners when dealing with people. Or anything else, for that matter.

First, the good news. The Cape buffalo is capable of running through virtually anything at speeds exceeding fifty kilometres per hour. This fact should convince you that you cannot outrun the buffalo once it decides it doesn't like you. It has excellent hearing, so don't make any noise when running away from it. Actually, it's no use running because the buff is going to catch you anyway. It has nostrils with the capacity of an industrial vacuum cleaner, and it can suck in your smell from far away, even if *you* think you don't stink. When it catches up with you, it will terminate your earthly sojourn by staving in your chest so that it looks like a ruptured barrel of herring, or by putting in plenty of horn where it hurts a lot. To make sure, it will roll over you like a black-tarred steamroller. R.I.P. (Rolled Into Pulp, if you didn't know.) So much for the good news.

Now, the bad news. Much has been written about the sheer tenacity to life of the Cape buffalo. Many stories exist about this magnificent game animal, which can reach nearly two metres at the shoulder and be three metres long. First imagine a tonne of steel-hard muscle, sinews like ship's hawsers, a tongue like a metal rasp, and lethal horns swept up and back, carried high on a powerful, thick neck. Add now a quick turn of speed and a total disregard for big bullets. Couple this with cunning, and you can see why the Cape buffalo fascinates hunters. Many have hunted *nyati* and have come off second best because they gravely (pun intended) underestimated the tenacity and cunning it is capable of developing when wounded.

Probably more ink has been splashed onto paper expounding on the shots to take and the bullets to use on *nyati* than for any other big-game animal. Much of that ink has now faded into dusty-smelling, crumbling, sepia-brown parchment, but the message is still valid today. Much lead has been shot at the Cape buffalo, too. Much of it has done the job very well. Some of it less well. Some has only served to get the hunter the undivided attention of a very angry buffalo. The latter scenario has already been eloquently written about by others; therefore the reader is spared the crawl through cruel thorns, following a gut-shot animal, the charge, and the rearranged anatomical details of the unfortunate recipient of *nyati's* bungling attempts at plastic surgery. Briefly, the best advice is, no matter what rifle and bullet combination you use, use it well. (The calibre .375 Holland and Holland Magnum, henceforth .375 H&H Magnum, is the minimum in most countries.) If you don't place your bullet well, you will get to know old *nyati* on his terms. For pure terror, you can't do much better than following up a wounded Cape buffalo. So much for the bad news.

Hunting the Cape Buffalo: He'll Scare You, Even When He's Dead

We had decided to hunt Cape buffalo in an area in the East Transvaal, now Mpumalanga (the land where the sun rises), South Africa. It was March, and unfortunately there were still plenty of leaves on the mopane bushes covering the block of land called "Rietvlei" on the Umbabat Reserve. Visibility was low, which is not a favourable setup if you intend to hunt dangerous game like the Cape buffalo. Too bad, we were here to do just that!

My professional hunter (or PH, from now on) and I finished our breakfasts, mopping up the salty black mushroom gravy that had accompanied the eggs and bacon with homemade bread. We drained our mugs of hot, sweet tea, laced with whisky, and we looked out over the bushland. Day was coming quickly, and the first pale blush of colour in the sky was brightening to the seduction of the sun. The far-off tops of the acacia and camelthorn trees had just started to break the skyline when the lanterns hissed their protest at being extinguished. We left the table, pausing only to snatch up a last piece of bread and butter. It might be a long day, and we had no idea when we would stop for a meal again. Our gear had already been loaded onto the Jeep by the two trackers, Peacock and Pius, who now sat quietly inside. They had wrapped themselves in woolen blankets against the chill dawn air and now looked like two black chrysalides waiting to hatch. I joined them in the back, and the hunt for a trophy Cape buffalo bull started.

One method of hunting Cape buffalo, because of the immense distances they cover in a day, is to drive along the dirt tracks and try to cut the spoor of a small group. The spoor found in this way usually belongs to bachelors known as *dugga* boys, and, for the most part, huntable specimens are found in such groups.

It was 8 A.M., and we had been searching the mopane bush for nearly two hours. Now, as we stood staring at the big tracks in the sand, waiting for our trackers to decide whether they were recent enough and whether the *nyatis* were the type we sought, I began, mentally, to run through the shot placement. I had decided to place the full-metal-jacket bullet low on the shoulder at close range, to get full penetration of the shot through the shoulder blade, lungs, and heart, to exit on the other side. I remembered tales of shot and wounded buffalo. Of hunters charged and killed. I knew that the first bullet must be deadly, and that it is worth everything else you might do later with follow-up shots.

The problem with Cape buffalo is that, after they have been shot, the adrenaline level in their blood rises and they do not register any additional bullets. They become sort of punchdrunk, developing an extreme resistance to bullets, and that makes them very difficult to kill. At this point a brain shot is basically impossible, for not only is the brain well protected under a thick horn boss and a skull like reinforced concrete, but when *nyati* comes for you, he will come at a stiff-legged gait and keep his head up high. He will keep you well in sight and drop his head (making for a clear shot) only at the moment of contact with you—and by this time, you're done for. Remember that a good buff will weigh at least ten times more than you do. That mass, applied to your backside at fifty kilometres per hour, is a crushing blow to your ego—and whatever else you may have left after a close encounter with *nyati*.

My thoughts were interrupted as I registered Peacock's thumbs-up sign; we were on to a group of *dugga* boys, at last! Grinning and exposing white teeth in shiny ebony faces, they now beckoned us onto the spoor. The trackers were like bloodhounds, pausing now and then to examine a piece of chewed grass or to test the consistency of the dung that lay along the spoor. Pius stopped and dipped his fingers into a pouch made from the scrotum of a long-dead *nyati* and extracted a pinch of fine wood ash, which he let fall. The white powder drifted with the wind, showing that our scent was being carried away from the quarry. As we continued through the bush, we could see that the spoor was getting fresher. The sun had not had enough time to dry the bright greenish pancakes left by the buffaloes.

After an hour on the spoor, we could smell the rank odour of the *nyatis* in front of us; the wind was still being kind. Now and then, a cloud of white birds would fly up and leave their buffalo friends momentarily and then settle slowly back. They looked like the artificial snowflakes you see in those plastic globes filled with water and white bits that swirl when you shake the globe and settle slowly over a miniature plastic landscape. The cattle egrets provide a good lookout service for the buffalo. In return they get a meal, snapping up the insects disturbed by the beasts as they move along. We looked over the scene and worked out our strategy. We had to take care not to raise the suspicions of the feathered sentinels. We were aware that a slight shift of wind direction could precipitate a stampede, and we would either be charged or left only with buzzing flies after the dust settled. We were not prepared to accept a wasted day's stalking, so we continued to monitor the wind.

Suddenly, Peacock sank to his haunches and motioned, palm downward, for us to do the same. The eyesight of black trackers is acute, superior to that of the average white man. I squinted to try to see what had got his attention. The mopane bushes are still in leaf in March, and despite the ravages of millions of mopane worms (caterpillars that may be eaten as a rich source of protein), the visibility was still low, roughly twenty metres in all directions. My PH and I had sunk to our haunches and had moved up like gnomes to reach Peacock. He pointed to a small black patch through the green leaves and then moved behind us. I was on the left, and my PH was to my right. The buffalo was feeding and moving toward a small opening in the bush cover on the right. My PH had a better view than I of the *nyati* and assessed it to be a trophy bull; he gave me the sign to shoot. It was twenty metres away, broadside, and exposing its right shoulder to me.

The booming bark of the rifle ended the silence. For a second nothing moved, and then buffs poured out from behind every conceivable bush and tree, nook and cranny. The bull I had shot stood swaying as his system digested the meal of five thousand joules of kinetic energy I'd just fed to him via the full-metal-jacket bullet. I quickly placed a second piece of steel-nosed lead on his shoulder for insurance, and he staggered off into the mopane before I could deliver a third helping. In the meantime, the other buffaloes had run off, leaving only the fading sound of their drumming hoofs in the distance and the odour of their dung and clouds of fine floating dust. The dust irritated our eyes, making them red rimmed and itchy. I reloaded the rifle, smelling the pungent burnt-cordite tang of the bullet cases.

We waited five minutes, and then Pius and Peacock crept slowly forward, like schoolboys intent on mischief, to examine the spoor. Peacock showed where the bull had pulled his hoofs back into the sand upon receiving the bullet and then how the right foreleg had dragged across the ground as he moved off. We followed the bright lung-blood trail into a clearing where the buffalo was waiting. He stared at us with red, angry eyes, and, as he tossed his head, a torrent of blood left his nose and splattered onto the sand.

Giving a short *oomph*, *nyati* started his charge. I now felt like a skydiver who had just discovered that he had jumped out of the plane but had forgotten to pack his parachute. There was no going back. A wounded Cape buffalo is strictly a one-way affair. Either you get your ticket or he gets his. In the worst case, you can both end up leaving your bones to be bleached in the sun. The buffalo faltered, because of the broken right leg. My next bullet took him at the base of the neck, causing him to drop his head so that his nose touched the ground. Sand clung around his muzzle, sticking to the blood and mucus, and he remained there swaying before another bullet, through the top of the shoulders, killed him. Uttering the long and mournful *baawmooooo*, of the dying buffalo, *nyati* toppled over. He had given his farewell to the bush, his acknowledgment to death, and now lay still.

Reloading, for insurance, we went over to where he lay. The scabby, black body was scarce of hair, and remnants of *nyati's* last mud wallow clung in gray patches to his body like some pestilential skin disease. The base of his tail was spattered with caked dung and filth, and bunches of ticks nested thickly in the folds of skin around his scrotum like metallic blue and green grapes. He was crawling with vermin. The *nyati* was old, with a thick, evilly gnarled and riven jet-black boss to his horns that curved down before sweeping up to just the level of the boss. The worn and polished ebony horns ended in blunted tips that were still capable of being driven through anything.

My first bullet had gone through the right shoulder blade, punched a hole in the bottom of the heart, and exited the other side. The second had gone higher and farther back but had gone through both lungs and had also exited.

It was amazing that the animal had still been waiting for us, despite the damage inside him. With a horn span of 39 inches, the *nyati* just missed making it into Rowland Ward's book of trophy animals. I had a shoulder mount anyway, and to this day when I look at it, the massive boss and form of the horns *still* scare me. Yes, this old *nyati* demands as much respect in death as he did in life.

Chapter 2

Leopard
(*Panthera pardus*)

Leopards are still widely distributed in Africa and Asia. The amber cat with the black spots can live in many types of country but tends to follow humans and their animals—both of which can be potential food for *ingwe*. A fully mature male leopard will weigh in at over eighty kilograms, exceed half a metre at the shoulder, and stretch two and a half metres from nose-tip to tail-end. Leopards have immense strength and can carry a prey animal three times their weight up into a tree. Pound for pound they are probably the strongest of all land mammals. The black panther is the same animal as the leopard. The colour variation is due to genetic selection among leopards that tend to live more in dark jungles than open land. Leopards are solitary except when mating. The female stays with the cubs (up to four are born, about a hundred days after mating) until they are fully weaned and capable of hunting for themselves.

Leopards are opportunists and are very cunning. And dangerous. For example, the Rudraprayag leopard in India became an infamous legend as a result of its eight-year career as a people eater. At least 125 victims were killed and eaten by this cat before professional hunter Jim Corbett gave it heartburn and fatal indigestion via a big lead bullet, back in 1926.

Hunting the Leopard: Perfect Predator, Silent Stalker

The sun underwent its daily metamorphosis from a brilliant puddle of hot quicksilver, high in a cobalt blue sky, to a dull and cool orange ball, low in the darkening west. The night now came and hastily inked everything black in the lowveld in Mpumalanga, South Africa. Stars began to wink; the silence of a cemetery crept over the place. It was as if the bush had pulled a death shroud over itself and had died. The night is a time of sleep for some animals, but a time of wakefulness for others. A time to kill or to be killed. The endless struggle between the hunter and the hunted is never so manifest as at night. Night is the time of terror, where survival demands perfect stalking from the predator and fast reaction from the prey.

High up on an outcrop of rock, a predator of the night stared out, its pale, yellow-green feline eyes stabbing through the darkness. The old tom leopard turned its head slowly, taking in the scents through its flared nostrils and the faintest of sounds through its claw-torn, ragged-edged ears. It listened to detect both danger and prey. Satisfied, *ingwe* edged down from the rock ledge cautiously, favouring its right paw, which was swollen with pus. It had failed to take any prey two nights ago and, goaded by hunger, had tried its luck on a porcupine. The attempt had resulted in a few quills in the face and the one that now caused the festering in its paw. The cat stopped momentarily, to squirt a boulder with pungent cat urine. A breath of time later, it vanished silently into the bush.

The farmer had established his herd of cattle twenty years ago. Coming with his family from the cold, windswept Great Karroo in the South West, he had struggled to make an existence from the reluctant land. He had broken the terrain to the plough and had cleared the bush and planted maize to augment the fodder for his beasts. This year had been as hard as any other, and the financial outcome was always the same: just in the red, despite the hours of toil. He had harvested his largest maize field and had now led his cows and their calves onto the reaped expanse to clean up the grains left behind by the harvester. He watched them for a while, to see them settle down to their task, and then he left them to the night. He wasn't concerned about them; the big prides of lions had been shot out long ago, and he'd not yet lost any beasts to predators, or many to theft or illness. He was aware that *ingwe* shared this land with him, for he had found the spoor often enough, but he reckoned that there were still enough baboons, impala, and steenbok around to keep a leopard fed. The farmer hated baboons and shot them on sight. However, they had learned to recognize his vehicle and knew the distance at which a bullet would not present a danger. The baboons destroyed the farmer's crops and broke into his outhouses, or rondavels, pulling the thatch out of the roof and then defecating all over. Also, he'd seen the cunning creatures wait for impala ewes to lamb. At the moment of birth, when the ewe was at her most vulnerable, they would scamper up to her in a crablike gait, rip the lamb away, and start biting the wet, flaccid meat.

The full moon had now risen to bathe the bushland with soft silvery light. *Ingwe* made his way toward the stream where the gin-clear water tinkled and murmured gently between the stones, and green weeds waved sinuously, like belly dancers, to the music. Trying to slake the feverish thirst caused by its suppurating paw, the leopard lapped up the cool liquid, attempting also to fill its empty stomach at the same time. It stopped and listened for a heartbeat of time, and then it moved off as slowly and silently as a shadow creeps along the ground.

Ingwe approached downwind from the cattle and took in the bovine smell. It could easily make out the shapes of the massive humpbacked animals spread over the field. Some cows were standing; others were lying down, chewing their cud. It watched them. The calf it had selected had separated from the rest and was unaware of the *ingwe,* which had now moved in nearer. The leopard crouched lower in the grass until it became only a flattened shape. Edging nearer, it became a suggestion of a shadow sliding across the ground.

The *ingwe* had now crept to within twenty metres of the calf. Its back feet were bunched up beneath it, its claws unsheathed and fixed into the ground for purchase. In a lightning flicker burst of speed the cat launched itself. In less than two seconds its crochet hook claws were fixed deeply into the calf's shoulder, and its fangs were clamped like a vise into its throat. Its hind feet, armed with razor-sharp yellow sickles, were already viciously raking the calf's flanks and finding purchase. The prey had time to let out only a short bawl of surprise before the leopard's teeth penetrated its windpipe and pierced the jugular vein. The calf's life began to squirt in great warm bloody gouts directly into the mouth of the leopard and then to drip down onto the ground.

The leopard clung on like a great writhing gold and anthracite speckled leech. The rest of the cattle, hearing the commotion and picking up the taint of the predator on the air, stampeded away with wide-eyed terror, splattering dung below tails held high. The calf struggled to stand, but the loss of blood and the weight of the leopard caused it now to splay its legs and to stagger like a drunkard. Its life was ebbing away. As if in slow motion, the calf and leopard sank together slowly onto the ground. The calf fought again to get up but, with a violent shudder, fell down. Kicking feebly, it let out the strangled gurgle of a death rattle as its life was snuffed out.

The leopard now began to pull and jerk its kill to the cover of the bush. Normally the leopard would have dragged it to a convenient tree and, exhibiting an incredible turn of strength, carried it to safety, well away from hyenas. This leopard would have to appease its hunger on the ground because of the corruption in its paw. Now under cover, it first slit open the calf's belly and began to feed.

The silent time before real dawn came, and the sun had already stabbed a small hole in the sky, raising a bloody smudge in it, when the leopard got up from its meal. Most of the calf had been devoured. The predator stretched and looked around. Then it was gone. It would return.

The farmer and his helpers knew something was wrong when they came to the field. The cattle, all huddled together, were not feeding. The farmer counted them and then repeated his count. He confirmed the loss of a beast. He found and then followed the drag marks from the congealed pool of blood to where the leopard had left the half-eaten calf. The pug marks in the ground showed him where *ingwe* had lain next to the carcass and eaten. The farmer left his labourers to round up the remaining beasts. Grim faced, he drove away.

Most professional hunters consider the leopard to be the most dangerous and difficult to obtain of the Big Five game animals (elephant, rhino, Cape buffalo, lion, and leopard). Leopards are the essence of an enigma in their behaviour; their caution is as legendary as their boldness. Leopards may even run onto a *lapa* (the front stoop of a house), snatch up a sleeping dog (a favourite food, when they can get it), and bound off.

Usually timid, the leopard turns into a fiery package of pure spitting, slashing, biting fury when injured, and many professional hunters bear the scars to prove it. A wounded *ingwe* will wait until it is very sure it can nail (and tooth) you and then pop up from the clump of grass just in front of you, like some horrid jack-in-the-box—very bad news, because *ingwe* has a trick that it executes well before you know what's hit you. Securely hooking its back legs into you, it reaches over the top of your head and drives the claws of its front paw deeply into your scalp to make contact with the skull below. In one motion, like a can opener, it makes a trepanning cut and then lifts a flap of scalp off the top of your head and pulls this bloody curtain over your eyes. As can be imagined, the pain must be as bad as the fear that comes of not being able to see. During this time its back legs are pounding up and down on your abdomen like furry pistons, raking away both clothing and your sweet meat, slashing you open with scalpel-sharp hind claws. If you're not wearing thick clothing, such as a leather apron reinforced with chain mail, it may just succeed in disemboweling you. If it can get at your throat at the same time it's unzipping you, you've had your fatal overdose of leopard.

If you ever do manage to get an appointment at *ingwe's* exclusive hairdressing salon and, despite all odds, survive, your scalp, after being disinfected (I'll bet that will make your eyes water), can be put together like a jigsaw puzzle and duly sewn back on. Maybe you can have the part on the other side, if you ask nicely. It makes one hell of a toupee, almost as good as the real thing.

The tactic employed in leopard hunting depends on the fact that leopards will most often return the next night, to finish off the remains of a previous kill. Emphasis is placed on the words "most often," however, because leopards are wary, and if they suspect that something is wrong they will not come back. It is essential to realize that leopards have a very good sense of smell, excellent night vision, and even better hearing. The slightest nuance of unusual scent in the air, the smallest movement, and the faintest sound will all be unerringly picked up by this master predator. Once this occurs, the leopard will dissolve into the bush and avoid the place for a long time. Don't be too certain though; it might just have *you* on its menu tonight!

When hunting the leopard, remember the stories about its speed and ferocity. No matter how you imagine it, you will be surprised how quickly it appears and how quickly it leaves, either dead or alive, after having been shot at. Unless you crave for a new hairdo, make sure that you shoot straight. The classic way to hunt leopard is first to select trees, well apart from each other, preferably on or near the banks of a dry riverbed. The trees must be thick enough to allow the leopard to climb them easily, and there must be a slanting side branch to which a suitable bait animal can be securely wired. Consideration also must be given to the fact that leopards appear mostly in the last seconds of daylight. For this reason the bait tree must show the leopard up as a silhouette against the fading sunlight. The setup is arranged so that a feeding leopard will present itself broadside to the hunter waiting in the blind, usually less than fifty metres away.

The bait animal is usually an impala or a large warthog that has been slit open to expose the viscera. The bait is dragged about a mile in two directions to saturate the area with scent. The guts are then smeared on the trunk of the bait tree, and the bait is secured with wire along the length of the side branch. This is done to ensure that the leopard has to start eating the bait from one end and is restricted in its activity. The bait must be large enough so that the leopard has enough to feed on for one night and will still have enough to come back to the following evening. A baboon bait is usually devoured at one sitting and is therefore not suitable.

The baits are set out before noon and inspected early the following day. Usually, no bait is taken the first night because leopards prefer well-hung, ripened meat. Also, it is likely that a leopard has passed by the bait but was cautious about the setup and left. On the second or third day, if there are leopards in the region, a bait will be taken. The leopard is an opportunist and believes it has found the prey of another leopard. The spoor around the base of the tree and the fine hairs and claw marks on the tree will indicate the size and sex of the leopard. Signs such as large pug marks, well distanced from another, indicate a tomcat.

When there is a hit on the bait, the hunter builds a blind that will allow a clear shot as well as shield the hunter from the acute senses of the leopard. It is best to take the foliage for the blind from an area well away from the bait. Of course, the same types of foliage found in the area should be used, and all cutting or disturbance for about a mile around the bait must be assiduously avoided.

The distance of our blind from the remains of the calf was forty-five steps (about forty metres). The blind was assembled using soft iron wire to secure the main struts. Once it was in place and stiffened by side supports, foliage was draped over the entire structure, leaving only a tiny hole for the rifle and even smaller observation holes for the PH and myself. The blind completed, we left the area to verify the rifle's telescopic sight. One shot, from forty-five steps, at a tin can lid using a 300-grain softnose Silvertip bullet, in calibre .375 H&H Magnum, verified that the rifle was dead on. Now, it only needed luck—and plenty of it.

We entered the blind at four in the afternoon. We had blackened our faces to reduce the chance that *ingwe* would pick up a pale patch of movement in the darkness. We must have looked like fugitives from the "Black and White Minstrels Show" (my apologies to Al Jolson). The rifle was ready and resting on two forked sticks. A glimpse through the telescopic sight confirmed that the cross hairs were on the carrion (it had started to stink). The sky had already darkened when a baboon high up on a rock face let out a single sharp warning bark. This was immediately answered by others, and soon a cacophony of baboon cries could be heard. Was *ingwe* coming to supper?

The baboon noise abated, and we waited. Time moved as slow as molasses, and the carrion was now discernible only as a sombre patch on the dark ground. The tension in the blind was as taught as harp strings. We strained our ears against the snake-hissing sound of silence. Nothing. Suddenly, the foliage of the blind rustled, and a high-pitched *peeu, peeu, peeu,* broke the silence. The bushbaby (*Otolemur crassicaudatus*) peered down at us with its immense bug-eyes. Its ears twisted and curled in every direction like miniature flexible radar dishes, trying to pick up a sound from the creatures sitting below it. Bushbabies are harmless creatures, unless you happen to be a grasshopper or some other insect. They always remind me of gargoyles on a medieval church. With another sharp scolding burst of *peeu, peeu peeu!* the little creature leapt away into the bushes. Silence washed in over us again. We waited.

Staring at the dark area where the carrion was, I became aware that a lighter shadow had moved near to the carrion. Guess who had come for supper? Leopards have a way of just appearing such that you never hear them arrive. I eased the safety catch off the rifle and sought shadow on a black background. It was difficult. My eyes began to water at the effort, and twice I had to glance away to allow them to clear. I again found the shadowy form of the leopard. It stopped and stared at the blind, and I knew swooping gut fear. The black cross hairs of the telescopic sight dissolved in the dark shoulder of the leopard, and I started to squeeze the trigger.

The trigger mechanism slid the retaining catch away from the firing pin. For a fraction of a second, the pin was held on the tiniest knife edge of hardened steel, and then the resistance was overcome by the power of the spring. The pin slid from its precarious perch and slammed down sharply onto the soft metal cap covering the priming of the bullet, suddenly compressing the small charge of shock-sensitive powder within. The spark created by the release of this chemical energy leaped out into the nitrocellulose-filled cartridge case. The inside of the cartridge instantly became an incandescent ball of gas at a searing three thousand degrees.

The laws of physics being what they are, the pressure created inside the case was about thirty-eight hundred times greater than normal air pressure. Restricted by the surrounding support of the rifle's breech, the brass bullet case could not deform to accommodate the immense pressure within it. The 300-grain Silvertip bullet still remained crimped into the neck of the cartridge. However, the gas pressure at its base now started to overcome the seating and friction resistance that had formerly kept it in place. The bullet began to move out of its case like a rocket leaving its silo. Slowly at first, but gaining speed as each fragment of time passed, the bullet was suddenly free from its cartridge, floating on a cushion of white-hot gas at immense pressure. Now it slammed into the rifling of the barrel at nearly three times the speed of sound, or just under a thousand metres per second (that's about twenty-two hundred miles per hour)—fast by *any* measure. The bullet was moulded into the interior of the spiraled rifle barrel and forced to comply: It began to turn. The unrelenting force of the hot gases drove it down the barrel; it would twist three times around its axis before leaving the 61-centimetre barrel.

It now left the barrel, its skin lightly marked with the spiral rifling pattern one tenth of a millimetre deep. One fifth of a second had passed since the firing pin had struck the primer, and the bullet had now slowed to approximately two and a half times the speed of sound as a result of frictional losses. It was revolving around its longitudinal axis three thousand times per second. Spin imparts stability to a bullet, like a gyroscope, preventing it from tumbling nose over tail during flight. The bullet now had 40 metres to travel to reach its target.

Five-hundredths of a second later, the bullet reached the leopard's shoulder. The tip of the bullet, formed of aluminum alloy, protected the soft lead core beneath it. The aluminum started to flatten as it bored into the leopard. The tip flattened some more, and the bullet began to penetrate. As it progressed its tip expanded, assuming a form like that of a button mushroom. The copper alloy body of the bullet near to the tip also started to peel open, leaving sharp petals that cut through muscle and devastated bone. The bullet was going slower now, but still at just over twice the speed of sound: about seven hundred metres per second (fifteen hundred miles per hour).

Only now did the leopard hear the sound of rifle fire. It had not felt the bullet's contact, despite the fact that the projectile was now deep in its body and beginning to pierce its left lung. The bullet passed through this and then the other lung with hardly a check in its speed, these large organs being full of air. The bullet went on and through the rib cage and started to exit. Now, the leopard felt the great surge of internal pressure created in its body by the hydrostatic shock wave effect, the result of the virtual incompressibility of fluids. A fraction of a second later, the bullet for the second time pierced the thin skin, and now it ploughed into the ground behind the leopard. There had been a surge of pressure inside the leopard upon the bullet's entry, but, on the bullet's exit, there was now decompression. The shock caused *ingwe* to jump off to the right. Less than half a second had elapsed since I had fired the rifle.

I never felt the kick of the rifle, but I thought I heard the *dupf* of the bullet hitting. I did see a black smudge of shadow bound off. There wasn't a chance to shoot again. There never is. I sat in the blind already trying to reconstruct how it had been. We remained where we were, trying to hear any noise apart from the echo of the shot, bounding off the cliffs, and the baboons who were screaming abuse, as usual.

At a time like this you are alone. You have taken a shot at probably the most dangerous member of the Big Five; you may have wounded it, and you have put many people in danger. You feel the weight of your action pressing you down, robbing you of the confidence that you may have had about your shooting ability. You forget how you consistently put holes in paper targets at any distance. You were the best shot on the shooting range then. Everybody told you how well you did and what a great rifle you had and all that sort of thing and you loved it. You'd told your friends, whom you have now put into danger, "Just get that leopard on its kill, and I'll take care of business!" They believed in you as much as you believed in yourself. You now know that paper targets are the ultimate surrogates, sacrificially killed as substitutes for others.

You have let everybody down and muffed your shot and wounded that leopard at 40 metres. Now it's out there, just waiting to rip the face off anybody who gets near enough, and there's going to be hell to pay. You, as the trigger-squeezer, have lost *your* face, anyway. You have missed your shot. Goofed. Screwed it up. You watch your PH trying to smile and say by his actions, "Don't worry, I know we have it; it's just cleared off a bit and is lying dead, somewhere."

Lying dead? *Of course* it is—because you are the client, the one who brings the money in, and the PH has got to pay bills, too. You watch in the light of the torch how he wraps the woolen scarf around his neck and straps on the leather apron. He knows as well as you that you have wounded, not killed, *ingwe*. You try to say something about the shot, but your throat is dry and rough and you cover your croak with a throat-clearing cough. Your PH offers you a drink. You accept it, unconsciously categorizing it as a peace offering. You wish only that you'd never taken the shot.

The tracker has arrived at the blind and he has the hooded eyes of an African, not telling you anything. He doesn't have to. You know that he despises you for wounding. He has a wife and many children, and he knows that if *ingwe* gets him, life for them will be harder than death. Unspoken words of reproach are screamed although no sound is uttered. The PH and his tracker go about their business. You know that a PH will never allow his client to be exposed to danger, so you don't ask if you can come along. As if reading your mind, the PH will say that he would really like you there, but too many people around will cramp his style. After all, if the leopard needs the coup de grace (but it won't because he knows it's dead, he tells you), it will be easier alone. You want to believe him and you lie to yourself.

The penultimate act is when he tells you to stay put in the blind. The final act is when he pops two thick and ugly 10-gauge magnum shells into the short-barreled shotgun and snaps it closed. He has told you that the buckshot in there will stop a Cape buffalo and that it is all standard procedure in the case of wounded leopards. "You have to be quick and shoot'em like a pheasant," he adds. You know then that he doesn't believe that *ingwe* is dead and that he is trying to lessen the advantage that the leopard will have at bad-breath range. That sharp, mechanical click of the shotgun being closed serves to underline some kind of finality. You watch them leave.

You can see the beam of torchlight bobbing up and down through the bushes, casting weird dancing shadows that metamorphose into the shapes of attacking leopards. They have reached the carrion now, and, with the tracker on the ground and the PH covering him, the search for spoor, blood, and cut hair begins. They move off, shuffling along to their death or mutilation like condemned prisoners, the man with the shotgun following the black retriever. But this is no pheasant shoot, rather the follow-up of a wounded leopard. One hell of a difference. They vanish from sight as the bush crowds in, and then you are alone.

You see and hear nothing, and you sit there with your useless rifle clasped in your sweaty hands. You open the breech and remove the empty cartridge case and touch the cause of your misery. You put the spent shell into your pocket and touch other bullets there. They are startlingly cold; you remove one and insert it into the rifle. It is something to do. You wait and listen for cries of pain, shots, and snarls, but the bush is quiet. You glance at your watch but do not see the ghostly smears of the luminous hands and do not register the time. It is something to do. The urge now is to get out of the blind that is now serving as your isolation cell in purgatory. Your bladder feels as if it will burst, but still you remain sitting. You see the light returning. You fear the news, and then you register what your PH is saying: "We've got a difficult one here; afraid you took him a bit too far back. He left a bit of gut and blood for us to find, and now he's waiting somewhere and is very pissed off." You feel sickened to the core, sick for yourself and the friends whom you have put into danger. You feel sick for the leopard. It's lying up somewhere, fermenting its agony into a potent and deadly brew of anger and boldness as the black blood, mixed with the gut contents, swirls around in its belly.

"Well, let's wait a bit and then I'll go with Tschokwane and see what we have."

I started involuntarily as the voice of the PH broke through my thoughts. I came back to reality. Tschokwane, our tracker, had appeared after he'd heard the shot. We discussed the shot and agreed that it had been a difficult one, what with the poor light.

I waited in the blind and they left. My earlier thoughts and misgivings repeated themselves, and then my PH was back at the blind, slapping me on the back and shaking my hand. Tschokwane was grinning. He shook my hand in that awkward, thumbs-grabbing way that Africans have. I heard that the big tomcat was lying dead, not far away, with a hole in his left shoulder and a not-too-big but raggedy exit hole—one that any old taxidermist could fix—through the other side.

Leopard

The leopard was thin; the infected paw had become a lump of putrid meat. The leopard was about nine years old and measured 7 feet, 6 inches from the nose to the tip of the tail. The skull measurement, sixty days afterward, got him a permanent place in Rowland Ward's book.

Chapter 3

Elephant

(*Loxodonta africana*)

Great herds of elephant once roamed most of the African continent, where food and water—above all water—were available. Then came the white man, greed for land, loss of habitat, and the desire for the ivory that these largest living land mammals carry. The arrival of the modern high-powered rifle and, later on, the machine gun in the hands of poachers, has, in some places, made the existence of the elephant a tenuous one. This is especially so when no game management is practiced. Indiscriminate shooting by ivory hunters and poachers has mostly destroyed the social makeup of the elephant families, which are always led by a matriarch.

With elephant, the bull also has a reproductive cycle and comes into season, called musth. This condition is indicated by irascibility and a sizable discharge of fluid from the temporal glands. The bull will urinate copiously, and the penis will be distended enough to drag on the ground and leave a furrow on the spoor. Some plough! Mature bulls keep away from the family groups except when in musth. They will then join the group for a while to mate. Such bulls are dominant over those not in musth. Twenty-two months later, a single calf is born. Elephants live fifty years or more. Deep within the elephant brain there lives an awareness of death, and they will become disturbed at the sight of elephant bones. Very old bulls will turn into solitary animals as the evening of their life approaches; such bulls are huntable since they are no longer breeding. License fees are high for this legal hunting, but they are an essential source of income for game management and antipoaching programs.

Hunting elephant is dangerous. Many an unwary hunter has finished up doubling as a fly whisk after his head has been ripped off by an elephant's powerful trunk. Keep *your* head and shoot straight!

Hunting the Elephant: Trouble with Tobacco

The bull was old. Born more than fifty-five years ago in the bushveld adjoining the Kruger National Park, *ndlopfu* was now on his sixth and last set of molars. This meant he was on borrowed time; a maximum of three years to go before the hyenas would circle him, grinning wickedly. He was already finding it difficult to get enough tender shoots and bark to fill his cavernous stomach and had taken to pushing trees down to get at the few palatable and easily chewed leaves. He needed a fifth of a tonne of green and some seventy litres of water each day to keep his body functioning. The handicap of possessing an inefficient digestive system forced him to consume even more vegetable matter. Most of his food passed straight through, only partially digested. Despite this ever-increasing destruction of his habitat the bull had slowly been losing condition, and now his hide hung in loose sheets on his gaunt frame. With age, the bull had started to wander the old trails he'd known as a calf. He did this together with a younger bull, or askari (soldier). This is the way of the elephant.

The place was Umbabat, Mpumalanga, South Africa, the time of year was August, and the bush was in a sorry state. Scraps of leaves clung and trembled tenuously to the branches and wailed a keening dirge as the wind passed through them. The occasional dust devil chased over the sand like a spinning top, only to then run out of power and dump its burden of sand. . . . The skittish wind was not good, because we were hunting elephant, animals that have an excellent sense of smell. We were walking, realizing that you kill all game with a rifle but an elephant you kill with your feet. And I don't mean kicking him to death; you use your feet to walk, walk, and walk.

We had been following the elephant for some time, and the sun was already shimmering white and hot in the sky. We had picked up the spoor five hours earlier, leaving the water hole and heading into the mopane bush. Our tracker, Tschokwane, had brought us through the "miles of bloody Africa," as Ruark once put it, and we were fully immersed in a sea of brown leaves. The heat smashed down on us, and the wind blew like a hair dryer in our faces. The liquid in our water bottles would have doubled for Tabasco; it did little to ease our raging thirsts. Even the furrowed brow of old Tschokwane was beaded with sweat as we sat down to review the situation. The way of the elephant, he told us in his amusing mixture of English, Afrikaans, and Shangane, was to "move plenty at night, drink enough, all right in the morning, walk plenty before midday and sleep in hot hours, before move again." I noted bitterly, as a blister on my foot started to throb, that our particular elephant had really taken the "walk plenty" part to heart. The tracker assured my PH and me that the *ndlopfu* was, "just up the road now, resting." That this same statement had been made an hour ago didn't seem to worry him in the least, and he was eager to move again. We got up, shouldered our rifles, and took off after him. We had come to know this particular *ndlopfu* spoor well. The soles of the elephant's feet left a characteristic pattern in the sand.

Elephants have an excellent sense of smell and exceptional hearing to compensate for their weak eyesight. Consequently, the wind direction and silence must always be observed. Tschokwane stopped and poked a finger into a large round mound of dung, as a child will stick its finger into a cup of sherbet. He nodded with satisfaction. From the heat and moisture content he could tell how long ago it was since the elephant had passed this way. He murmured quietly that the *ndlopfu* could not be far ahead. He took out a leather pouch from the folds of his loincloth and shook from it a little of the wood ash that he collected every night from the campfire. The fine white powder drifted with the breeze and showed us that the erratic wind had now turned against us and must be bringing our scent toward the elephant. We made a wide skirting action, attempting to get our scent out of the direct line of the elephant and to head it off. We started the last phase of the approach but didn't realize, at the time, that we were going into danger.

The *ndlopfu* was leaning, resting under a huge *marula* tree. He had been here before, when the small, sweet, yellow fruits had fallen to the ground in their thousands, and he had eaten well. Later, when they had become overripe and fermented, he had also eaten, becoming mildly intoxicated. Now, in winter, the tree was bare of all fruit and leaves. The elephant's bony back sagged deeply in the middle and his hip bones jutted out from his frame. Every now and then, he flapped his ragged, vein-filled ears lethargically to cool his blood and to dislodge the swarms of biting flies. His small, rheumy eyes were mere slits, and salt tears seeped from out of the wrinkled corners. Countless tiny, stingerless mopane bees, crazy for the moisture, swarmed around the tears. The askari bull was a bit farther off to the side, as was its habit; it always kept the older bull company but remained well to the side and parallel to it. It was busy stuffing assorted twigs and dry leaves into its mouth. The old bull's tusks were worn down and heavily stained brownish black from vegetable juice. The left shaft of ivory was longer and thinner than the right, indicating that it was a "right-handed" elephant. The younger bull lacked the thickness and length of ivory but was in much better physical shape; its speed of reaction and strength were as good a weapon as any.

The askari was alerted by the call of a tick bird that was perched on its head. The askari stopped feeding, its trunk remaining midway between a branch and its mouth, and spread its ears wide and listened, head cocked. It then dropped the bunch of leaves, slowly raising its trunk to search the air for scent. It found one, and a second later it moved off silently. We had approached near enough to be able to see the gray mass of the old bull. The wind was good, and we closed to thirty metres.

I had loaded my rifle in calibre .375 H&H Magnum with 300-grain, full-metal-jacket bullets. My PH had a similar bullet of 450 grains in his .458 Winchester Magnum. Much has been written about rifles, calibre, and bullet construction, but hunting elephant is not solely a question of legality or calibre; the hunter must use the rifle competently, quickly, and accurately. An elephant gut-shot with a .460 Weatherby Magnum softnose bullet is more likely to give you problems than one shoulder-heart shot with a .375 H&H Magnum full-metal jacket or solid. It is not the calibre that counts, but the bullet placement (and construction). Use enough rifle, and use it correctly. In the case of elephant, it is only the precise brain shot that ensures instant death. Care must be taken not to shoot too high up on the head and into the honeycombed dome of bone there. A shot there will get you into trouble. Plenty of it. The brain is situated low and deep inside the skull, protected on all sides by thick bone. However, a full-metal-jacket bullet or a solid, placed on the line between the eye and ear slot, preferably back toward the ear, will ensure instant death. Although a shot to the shoulder-heart region, given the correct calibre, bullet construction, and penetration, will be fatal, the elephant is likely to run off and cause varying degrees of destruction before dropping. It is for reasons of ethics and safety that the only viable shot is the brain shot, either from the side or the front, between the eyes. Sometimes, however, the shoulder shot may have to be used.

We had reached a patch of mopane trees and were observing the *ndlopfu* through our binoculars. This was the one. I got ready for the shot and placed the cross hairs of the telescopic sight low on the level of the eye and in front of the ear flap, where it joined the head. As I started to squeeze the trigger, I felt a tap on my shoulder. My PH pointed. Unnoticed by us, the askari had converged on our position and was standing to our left about fifty metres away. His ears stood out like sails, and his trunk was a sinuous snake that danced and waved in the air, searching for our scent. He was looking for trouble.

The young bull knew that we were there but had not detected any movement or any more scent, since the capricious wind had now turned again in our favour. It was undecided what to do, and we heard a deep rumble as it communicated its unease to its companion. Outflanked, we were certain that we would have no chance to escape a double charge and started to retreat, keeping both rifles trained on the aggressive bull. It shook its head from side to side, dislodging great clouds of dust and flies. We were very impressed with the show but reckoned we'd seen enough of the dress rehearsal and left by the backstage door, without paying.

We had been lucky not to have been caught out by the elephants and to have been taken in a pincer action. We put a kilometre or so between us and them and sat down to unwind. The water from our water bottles now tasted like nectar, albeit hot nectar. Tschokwane started to roll a rough-looking cigarette from native tobacco that he rolled up into a piece of newspaper. He set the contraption alight and it belched a gray black cloud of evil-smelling smoke into the air. It stank like a steam locomotive burning old rubber tyres for fuel. We were still talking in muted tones when we heard a noisy trumpeting start up from where we had just come. It was no bushveld jazz band, either. The elephants had caught our scent, or more likely the acrid tobacco smoke, and were coming, trumpeting shrilly. Stopping only to snatch the obnoxiously olfactory fag ("cigarette" is too noble a word for it) out of Tschokwane's hand and to stomp it viciously into the sand, I snatched up my rifle, and we ran away from the noise.

We put several more kilometres between us and the peeved pachyderms. The late afternoon sun still had power in it, and the weight of our rifles seemed to grow with every step. Skirting a dried-up riverbed, we came to a slight rise in the terrain and could see the immediate area around us. Scanning with our binoculars, we picked up the elephants as they moved through the bush. With their trunks upraised like periscopes they looked like great gray submarines wallowing in a sea of dead leaves. Checking the wind, we found that we were now well to the side of them, and it seemed also that they had stopped hunting for us.

It was getting late, so we gave up and made our way back to the Jeep. It was nearly dark by the time we found it. I am always amazed at the sense of direction that trackers have. I was lost until I saw the ghostly gray-white of the vehicle loom up suddenly in front of us. After removing piles of ghastly, tarry baboon excrement from the hood, we drove off. That night I couldn't sleep; the spectre of great gray beasts running me down was too vivid. It felt like only five minutes later when my PH came for me to go a-hunting again.

We found the elephants' spoor later on in the day. Learning from our previous experience, we fanned out and cut the smaller spoor of the askari, eighty or so metres to the left of the old tusker's. So, we noted, they were still keeping to their old trick, which very nearly had us done for the previous day. Following in a spread-out formation, we made quick progress with a favourable wind. Spoor and dung were getting fresher. Tschokwane scrambled up a tree and scanned the bush. He found the elephants about a kilometre away and we closed in. Bearing well to the right, to get us nearest to the old bull, we could now make out its gray shape, moving between the scrub and thornbushes. The wind still held in our favour, and we were able to get ahead of the bull. The distance was now about forty metres, and we were closing in well. Soon it would be a time to shoot, a time to kill, and a time to die.

I reached a gnarled *rooibos* tree. Using the telescopic sight at the lowest magnification, I searched out the killing spot on the elephant's head. The bull had stopped eating and turned slowly in my direction. Holding steady on the *rooibos* tree, I found the place for the side brain shot and squeezed the trigger. The bull's back legs immediately shot out from behind, and the beast crumpled up and dropped onto its right side with a crash like a felled tree. The bullet had penetrated all the way through the brain case and had exited the other side. Death had been instantaneous. Death, the leveler, in the raw. We remained where we were, knowing that the young bull was near; we wanted to avoid being charged or having to shoot another elephant in self-defense.

The sound of the shot thundered away over the bush. Then we heard the sharp cracking noise of trees being snapped off; the askari bull was running away. Tschokwane quickly went up a nearby tree and followed the bull's progress. He was running away, living to fight another day.

We went to the bull. The elephant had fallen on the side where the bullet had entered. The exit hole on the other side of the skull was now the source of a river of blood that meandered down the elephant's cheek and into the sand. Its hide was deeply creased and its ears were ribbons of skin because of the years of contact with the thorns of the bush. The right tusk had been forced deeply into the sand by the weight of the falling beast. The left one was worn and cracked. They had a dirty whitish yellow colour caused by the accumulation of vegetable juice stain over the years. After taking some photographs, we used the walkie-talkie to call in the meat processing team.

Nothing goes to waste in game management programs. Within two hours, despite approaching darkness, a team of twenty-five people had assembled around the elephant, and the butchering began. His great gray body slowly dissolved under the relentless onslaught of the axes and knives. We kept the skull, ears (for tabletops), tusks, feet (for stools), tail (for the wirelike hairs), and the hide (for leather). The meat was to be processed and sold to the locals. The task was completed, under the light of vehicles' headlamps and handheld torches, toward midnight. The lights caused the eyes of the gathering packs of hyenas to glow and dance like fireflies in the bush, as they sought for a position to be first in to clean up the remains. As we moved out, they came in. We saw hunchbacked forms gliding and ghostly in the torchlight. By morning, the great pile of elephant entrails and associated slop would be gone; this is the way of the *mpisi*.

Tschokwane was a changed man after the hunt; he seemed taciturn, sullen, and withdrawn, and he answered in few words questions put to him. With much coaxing we were finally able to draw it out of him. He was upset because I had snatched his fag away from him the day before (and they say that elephants never forget!). Searching in my bags, I found a couple of packets of duty-free cigarettes, and I gave them to him. He brightened up immediately and was rapidly his old self again.

The next day I noticed that he was still puffing away at his homemade fags, and I asked about the cigarettes I had given to him. He smiled broadly, exposing big chipped false teeth embedded in badly fitting, bright pink plastic gums, and told me: “Eh, this whiteman cigarette plenty fine; I sold ’em and can buy enough blackman tobacco. It’s all right.” Pressed further about the quality of the smokes he made compared with that of the bought product, he observed in an incredulous tone: “Eh, I’m telling you straight, that whiteman tobacco, it’s all right, Suh, but that t’ing can’t get elephants running. Blackman tobacco *plenty* fine for this!”

Elephants: And What’s More

The bushveld is a deserted place, and you would think that communication would be difficult; it is not. The existence of the “bush telegraph” makes it possible to exchange news and add lies ad libitum for those interested in such activities. Let me explain. It was known generally that I was in the area, hunting elephant. I had shot my bull the day before, and that was also common knowledge. The following will illustrate just how inventive waspish tongues can be.

We were driving along in the Jeep, hoping to spot an impala for rations. Peacock, another of our black trackers, suddenly tapped on the roof and hung over to tell my PH that there were many lions feeding on something, over to the right. My PH slowed down, and we could now see about seven lions feeding on a dead elephant. The bush area surrounding the carcass had been smashed down; sizable trees had also suffered, and their broken limbs glared whitely like bones.

We circled the pride of lions. They watched us. The stench of the sun-ripened elephant carcass, which had been opened up belly first by the cats to allow access to the entrails, was overwhelming. The situation became clear when we saw that the elephant’s tusks were still embedded in its skull; this was definitely not the work of poachers.

Furthermore, we could see no tracks from human feet around the area, and only great circles of elephant spoor were present. My PH backed the Jeep off and we returned to the lodge (one hour's drive), where we telephoned for the police and the nature conservation authorities. The telephone was a party line, and so the "silent listeners" were able to capture this piece of information. The authorities arrived in due time, and we went back to where the elephant lay. Making plenty of noise, we drove off the cats and then examined the area. A look at the many and big double puncture holes gaping in the side of the pachyderm verified that it had been killed by another elephant. The dead one was a young bull, and it had probably upset another bull, resulting in death. The case was registered as such, and we all drove off.

The next day we heard that it was already common knowledge in the bush that we had first shot a *small* elephant. Being disappointed with its ivory, we had left it to go and find a better one. . . .

Elephants: And Finally . . .

My PH also had a few tales about macho types who "hunt" to show off. One of his favourite stories was about a hunter who weighed at least 150 kilograms, a lot on anyone's scales. I never asked the name or nationality of this trencherman; I know that my PH would never tell me, as it is a PH code of honour never to speak about clients. During an elephant hunt, the man was so scared that when they got up close he messed up his shot. The result was a wounded elephant—the shot was through the trunk, painful but not deadly. The elephant trumpeted enough to shake the leaves off the trees and ran off, leaving my PH the chance of a snap shot as it quartered away. The "hunter" was so scared that he messed up himself as well as his shot: He lost control of his bowels. After some tracking, the PH was able to kill the elephant. He then had to send a tracker back to the Jeep to get paper, so that the "hunter" could clean himself up. After this, the immense man insisted that he be lifted up onto the dead elephant (he couldn't climb up unaided), where he posed proudly, arms akimbo, for photographs with his elephant.

Chapter 4

Lion
(*Panthera leo*)

A mature male lion will weigh around 250 kilograms and stand more than a metre at the shoulder. The lionesses are smaller, and they do most of the hunting. Mating takes place with dominant males only, and up to six cubs are born, about four months later. Lion cubs are in danger when a new male comes into the group, because his first interest is to kill them. This will bring the lionesses into heat, and the new male can then bring his genes into the group. Of all big cats, lions are the most sociable, and prides of up to ten adults plus young are common. Lions can live for twenty-five years.

If you didn't already know it, lions are very partial to anything on the meaty side of life. This ranges from live animals to putrid carrion. They will eat virtually anything. Lions can also develop an epicurean taste for Homo sapiens of all colours and races. This trait was amply exemplified by the two rogues of Tsavo, a very gifted duo of male lions that ate and digested a few hundred railway workers during their culinary career. Their activities were stopped in 1899 by J. H. Patterson, when he fed the man-eaters some high-speed lead bullets.

Hunting the Lion: Trouble with Fat

The lioness had now moved upwind to let her scent drift to the Cape buffalo herd. The other members of the pride were in position downwind, waiting. The feline predator's scent reached the moist, flared nostrils of the cow buffalo. She was heavy with calf, and she moved off immediately, communicating the bad news to the others in the herd. The unrest was contagious; the herd stampeded away, bellowing. The cow crashed through the bush and straight into the waiting jaws and claws of two lionesses. They went into action like a well-practiced team, the larger lioness going in low, under the neck, and hooking the butter-yellow dew claws of her front paws into the cow in a deadly embrace. It then clamped its fangs into her throat, blocking her air. The suffocation phase of the kill had started.

The other lioness leaped onto the buffalo's back and drove its sickle claws deeply into the black hide. The back legs came up and found purchase. The larger lioness hung onto the buffalo, using her weight to drag down the prey. The combined weight and strangulation began to show effect. Other lions then appeared from out of the bush, biting at the cow's legs, hamstringing it, and hanging onto its tail with a jerking-tugging action. The buffalo staggered along but had no chance against the overwhelming odds. It went down and, still alive and kicking feebly, it was ripped open. The cats started feasting. By this act, the lions had just filled all the requirements to become classic "nuisance animals." They would have to be killed, either by the government agency or by a paying hunter. In any case, the outcome for the lions would be the same.

Lion

We were hunting in the Mica area of Mpumalanga, South Africa, when we heard about the pride of lions that had taken a partiality to Cape buffalo meat. The buffaloes were on private land, where they had been resettled as disease-free breeding stock. Such predations on these valuable game animals were intolerable, and thus the lion pride was destined to be shot out. This sort of hunting, for which the hunting client must pay a hefty trophy fee, helps to ease the financial loss to the farmer without costing the authorities anything in compensation. The client has the satisfaction of the hunt and the knowledge that he has eased the financial burden on already depleted public funds, thereby allowing them to be used for conservation purposes. I was just such a client.

My tracker and I stood looking at the carnage in front of us. The buffalo was a shell of bones to which shreds of skin and meat were still attached. Squadrons of metallic green flies buzzed and patrolled over the carcass whilst others crawled over it, laying bunches of banana-shaped white eggs on the remaining meat. Maggots were already working under the flaps of skin, causing it to undulate as if it possessed a life of its own. Vultures circled high in the sky, black gliders waiting their turn to drift down and finish off the rest. The stink from the carrion was overwhelming, and we had to force down our rising bile and get upwind from it. Our usual tracker, Peacock, a considerable lady's man, was not with us. He had taken a day or two off to, as he put it, "lie with" some of his wives. We had another helper that week, a small black imp named Andrees. This man hailed from Mozambique and belonged to the Shangane tribe, which has its roots in the Zulu nation. He was an excellent tracker who went regularly back to Mozambique, using the Kruger National Park as a shortcut. The distance he traveled was about one hundred kilometres over a land crawling with all sorts of creatures that crave meat, human included. The small Shangane studied the tracks and told us that there were five lions, one of which was certainly a big male.

The rest of the day was spent looking for a suitable bait animal in the form of a broken-down zebra. The aim of the exercise was to remove problem lions, so we had to act quickly and not wait until the lions had another chance to kill a buffalo. We found a suitable zebra very late in the day and converted it into lion food with a shot to the shoulder. We first slit its belly open. The "striped donkey" was then dragged a circuitous way toward a place where we would be able to see whether the cats were feeding and make the best approach. We placed our offering at the base of a tree, near to the remains of the buffalo. We fixed it securely with a thick metal chain because we didn't want the lions to drag it off. We wanted them to eat where we could see them all and be able to have a clear shot at the lion selected. We pulled a heavy leafy blanket over the zebra, to protect it from vultures and hyenas, and left.

Night came, and the sky became jeweled with heaven's diamonds. On earth, the shadows lengthened and merged with each other and crept along the ground, laying a thick, black, velvet carpet over the bushveld. The lions stirred and stretched the sleep out of their muscles. They then began to search for meat.

The sun had already burnt off the last scraps of mist hanging on the Drakensberg Mountains, far off to the west, as we sat down to breakfast. We had black bread, impala liver and kidneys, and fried onions. It went down well, aided by piping hot sweet tea laced with whisky. My PH was confident that the bait would have been found and, with luck, the lions would still be feeding or lying up nearby, to keep the hyenas away. I was to use my favourite rifle, a repeater in calibre .375 H&H Magnum. I slid two 300-grain Silvertip bullets into the magazine and put another in the chamber. The safety engaged automatically. My PH checked his rifle and loaded it in .458 Winchester Magnum with heavy, softnose bullets. He snicked the safety on and we went in the Jeep to see if any big pussycats had come to dinner last night.

We saw them at some distance: black specks of vultures already circling high in the blue sky. As we approached the bait area we saw other vultures sitting hunchbacked in the trees. They twisted their heavy, beaked, and bald heads, supported on red scrawny necks, to examine us. I had the distinct feeling that they were weighing up their chances for an extra bit of meat after the lions finished with us. After having assessed us, they flapped heavily off the trees to join their black brethren up on the thermals. The fact that they were not on the ground indicated that other visitors were at the bait.

Andrees was the first to spot the lions. They were lying up, lethargic, sun-dappled, and golden under the shade of a tree, their bodies bloated with meat. The old male lion was behind the pride, partially hidden by bush. We could make out that its mane was thin, typical of the rangy lions in this part of Africa. You rarely get to see a lion in the bushveld as handsome as the one that roars at the start of an MGM film. Life here is harder than in Hollywood, or so they say, and most male lions in the bush lose their manes. Lions living on the more open plains tend to keep their hair.

We were about fifty metres away from the pride, and one lioness stood up and turned to face us. Her tail twitched from side to side, indicating that she meant business; we retreated. We drove off to wait for the lions to settle down to their siesta again. After an hour, we had hatched out our plan of attack.

We took about half an hour to crawl to the lions. They were lying around randomly, as if someone had dumped heaps of tawny-coloured sand on a building site. They had long forgotten our earlier intrusion and were asleep. Only the occasional flick of a black-tipped tail indicated that there was any life in the beasts before us. Andrees had melted into the cover and was finding out where our quarry was.

He soon came back, eyes glittering, and beckoned us to follow. We crawled for another eternity and then we saw the male lion standing up, urinating. I reckoned the distance to be thirty-five metres. Close enough in anyone's book. Since the lion stood facing me, my only option was a chest shot. The cross hairs of the scope went onto the spot well below the chin but above the curve of the front legs as they come from the chest. As I was lying down, I could support the rifle well. I squeezed off the shot. *Bang-thduk*. Bullet contact had been established.

The lion flipped over as if poleaxed and lay still, except for the nervous reaction of its tail, which thrashed at the ground like a writhing snake. The other lions sprang to their feet and stood their ground, snarling about their rudely disturbed sleep, no doubt. Their agitation was clearly reflected in the way that their tails whipped back and forth. We retreated slowly, on the lookout for a charge, but none came; maybe they had eaten too much. We got back to the Jeep and decided to return using the protection of the vehicle. The bush was thick, and we didn't really know how many cats were crawling around in there. We *did*, however, know the sort of mood that they were in.

Rifles were checked and we made our approach. We took a direct route and soon we were near enough to see the dead lion. We couldn't see any other lions and so drove up to the dead one. Satisfied that he had left this life, and the others had left the place, we got off the Jeep and began loading up. A mature lion is quite a weight, dead or alive. I'd shot a very mature one. As we were debating how best to get it onto the back of the Jeep, we heard a short grunting sound. We turned to see a lioness by a clump of bush. She was watching what we were doing with her old man, and she didn't approve. Our rifles were close at hand and we quickly had the sights on her. We were reluctant to shoot, however, because we had only one license, which was already used up, and the authorities are not easily convinced that you shot in self-defense. I suppose that they might believe you, though if you were brought in alongside your lions with your throat opened up, revealing your now nonpulsing jugular vein.

It was clear that the lioness didn't want her old man taken on any outing to the taxidermists, and she stood her ground in a half-crouching stance. She was ready to charge. Somewhere in the distance, a zebra hee-hawed like a demented jackass, and this distracted the lioness. She half-turned her head. Seizing the initiative, my PH fired a bullet directly in front of the cat, spraying sand at her. She left. We got her old man nicely loaded into the back of the Jeep and drove off with him. We left the lioness to get on with life as a widow, but we knew that another male would soon take over.

As we drove home, the lion's head nodded to the bumps on the track, and a trickle of blood now came from the hole in its chest; there was no exit hole. We arrived at base camp, and helpers loaded the lion off and into the skinning shed. Although it was getting late, the skinners started their work with enthusiasm. I was surprised but attached no meaning to it.

The bullet had gone into the chest, shredding the heart and shattering the lungs, going on to break the spine halfway down its body. It had stopped just under its skin, from where it was removed by a skinner. He handed it to me. I tipped him five US dollars. An expensive bullet. It was now like a metallic flower: The tip had peeled back into four razor-edged petals, and the stem had retained its stubby form, marked only by the imprint of the rifling.

Lions, as well as leopards, have a special trophy in addition to their hide, skull, and dew claws. Deeply embedded into the muscles of the shoulder, one on each side, are the "floating bones." They are a hockey-stick shaped curiosity not attached to the skeleton, and they can be made into a piece of jewelry. Witch doctors use them in their bone bags when predicting the future, and as such they are a sought-after commodity. The floating bones were removed and cleaned, and I took possession of them, just in case they became “lost,” somehow, during the night.

The helpers were also very quick to strip off the great lumps of rancid yellow fat from the lion’s body as it became exposed during the skinning process. This material was packed into plastic bags, rolled-up paper, and strips of cloth and triumphantly carried away. I was surprised at this behaviour but would find out only the next day just what this was all about.

The next morning something was wrong. I lay in bed listening, trying to hear what was going on, and then I realized—it was the silence that was wrong. Usually, at this time of day one would be awakened by the tea boy or by the noise and clatter of people going about their jobs or getting ready to go hunting. Today there was silence. I dressed and noted that the water bowl was empty, another sign. Stepping out of my tent I saw my PH. He was upset.

“The boys have all cleared off home, and we won’t see them until they’ve had their fling.”

“What do you mean?” I asked, in the bewildered and dry-throated croak of the sleepy, thirsty, and unwashed.

“It’s as simple as a pimple! Yesterday you killed a lion, and that is mighty medicine. Didn’t you see them, stripping off the lion fat like shelling peas?”

“Yes, but what’s all that to do with the fact that the camp’s deserted, except for us two?”

“Everything,” he replied. “They believe the stuff can cure anything from gonorrhea to gut-ache. They also swear that they can sire male babies after a good rubdown with lion fat, and they’ve gone home to try the bloody stuff out! I’ll bet that they’ve been going at it like rutting stags all night, knocking up their women. They will be good for nothing, if and when they come back.”

So, that was it. That’s why they were so enthusiastic to skin late last night. I turned to my PH.

“Well, let’s hope that they are in fair enough shape when they do come back, otherwise there’s going to be hell to pay." I added, facetiously, "I am already planning to deduct your daily PH rate."

"Tell you what," he said, pretending not to have heard, "let's spend a day or two shotgunning for birdies instead of this dreary big-game stuff. It'll fill in the time nicely, until our lusty lads come back."

He had struck the right note with me because we hadn't eaten guinea fowl or francolin for at least a week, and a change from impala and warthog was long overdue.

Two days later, the first of the Romeos strolled into the camp, grinning self-consciously. Their black faces beamed with suppressed mirth as they were admonished by my PH and told of the cuts in pay and rations and other sanctions that would be forthcoming. It must have been worth it, because they continued smiling. More errant lads came trickling back during the third day, and by day four no more were missing. We could go hunting for big game again. Despite everything, the first thing we did was to shoot a warthog for our helpers, telling them to fill their bellies, as they were certainly in need of strength-giving food after their strenuous "holiday." This remark caused them much mirth. They even tried to out-eat each other, to show how "busy" they had been.

Chapter 5

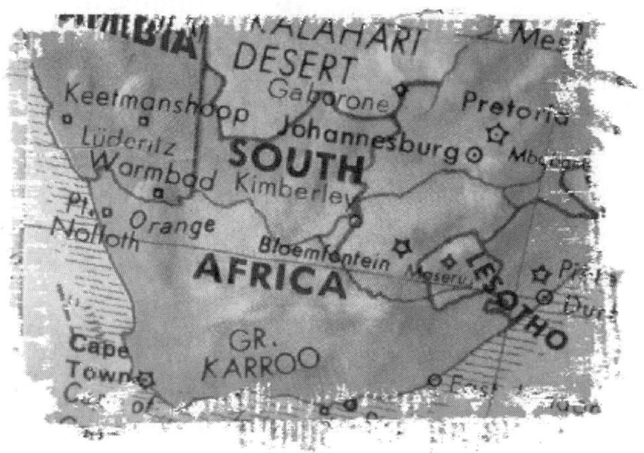

Southern White Rhinoceros

(*Ceratotherium simum simum*)

There are five known species of rhino in the world today, namely the African (two species), Indian (about two thousand left), Sumatran (about four hundred left), and Javan (about fifty left). In Africa, the two species are the black and the white rhino. The quick to charge and cantankerous black rhino (about two thousand of which are left) is a browser, feeding off shoots and leaves (including semipoisonous ones), and has a prehensile lip. It is not sociable, except when breeding, when it also fights like hell. Despite the nuptial strife, they do get around to mating. The calf usually runs after the cow. The black rhino is threatened with extinction.

The less evilly disposed and slightly less likely to charge white rhino is much larger than the black. A bull may tip the scales at over three and a half tonnes and stand two metres at the shoulder. It will reach four metres in length; the front horn can exceed a metre. The second horn is usually smaller, but both horns can put a big hole in you. The white rhino is a grazer with a square mouth and adapted lip configuration. Ecologically, it opens up short grass grazing areas, helping animals that prefer short grass to crop. It is a social animal, and family groups are usual. The calf usually leads the cow. Its name has nothing to do with its colour. It got the name "white" from a South African Boer word, *wyt*, meaning *wide*, describing the mouth. Any rhino adopts the colour of the last mud wallow it was in. So much for the linguistic abilities of the English.

The white rhino has two subforms or species, the northern (thirty of which are left, and it is clearly threatened with extinction) and the southern. The southern white rhino is not currently endangered with extinction (about seven thousand are left, and its numbers are increasing), and limited trophy hunting is allowed. The considerable fees generated for this privilege are ploughed back into rhino management schemes. The southern white rhino's recovery from near extinction and its management to a viable species is a great tribute to the game management efforts of the South African government.

During the 1800s, considerable numbers of white rhino populated the southern tip of Africa. The opening up of the land marked the start of the slaughter campaign to rid the land of all large, dangerous game (rhino included) and to replace it with cattle. By the beginning of the 1900s only a handful of rhinos existed, in a tiny reserve called Umfolozi, in Natal Province. With great care, expense, and protection, the rhino started to make a recovery. Relocation was done when the habitat was secure, and slowly the numbers swelled. Breeding herds were established, and, at the end of 1990, some ninety years after the near-extinction, the population is viable. And that does not take into account breeding successes in other lands. Game hunting, under the strict control of government agencies, provides the much-needed financing for a continued success story. Only about one percent of the total white rhino population in

South Africa is hunted for sport, but the revenue generated thereby guarantees the existence of the rest.

The main problem of the rhino family lies in the fact that they carry a liability on the end of their nose. Incidentally, the horn is not part of the skeleton; it is attached to the outside skin, somewhat like a wart. Rhino horn (both the black and white rhinos have two horns, one behind the other) has long been used in Far Eastern medicine. Although the actual therapeutic effects of the horn, which is made of keratin (a protein found in hoof and hair), may be minimal or dubious, the psychological effect is apparently great.

The other much-touted effect of rhino horn, namely as an aphrodisiac, is not proven scientifically. It is a biological fact that when mating, the rhino is capable of multiple copulations, but this has nothing to do with the horn on its nose. Rhinos that have been captured, dehorned, and then released by the authorities in antipoaching programs have not changed their mating habits. In addition, old rhinos might still have plenty of horn but will no longer breed. For me, at least, this indicates that there is no relationship between the presence or absence of a rhino's horn and the rhino's sexual behavior. I fail to see how consumers of rhino horn can relate their sex lives to that of rhinos, anyway.

The southern white rhino is a Big Five animal. Rhinos have an immensely tough, thick skin and heavy bone structure. This requires a calibre of at least .375 H&H Magnum (legal minimum), a full-metal-jacket or solid bullet of suitable construction, and a well-placed shot. A softnose bullet will mushroom on the iron-hard, callused skin and cause a stinging but superficial wound. Believe me, rhinos don't like that at all. Given that they have been clocked at over fifty kilometres per hour over a short distance, no one can outrun a rhino. The size of the animal leads one to think it is slow and cumbersome. Wrong. It is quick and as agile as a flea, and it can stop dead and run off at another angle in a short distance and in even less time.

The best bullet placement is the side brain shot at close quarters. An imaginary line, drawn from the eye level to the lower ear, crossing another imaginary line drawn vertically from the ear, and a bit forward and up, is a good spot. The brain shot from the front is made when the rhino charges, but this requires fast, precision shooting to avoid bullet deflection by the horn, or, worse still, hunter deflection by the horn. Not recommended in either case. Another shot placement, low on or just behind the shoulder region, demands deep penetration of the bullet through bone. Although heart-shot, the rhino may run off before dying. The hearing and sense of smell of rhinos are excellent. This seems to compensate, in part, for their notorious shortsightedness. They can see only up to about twenty metres but can register movement well.

Hunting the Southern White Rhino: A Close Shave or Two

It was in April and the start of winter in an area near Hoedspruit in South Africa. The property that we were hunting on had a good number of rhino. The old bull rhino that we were seeking had been established on the property many years ago. It had bred successfully but had now become solitary. The decision was made to hunt it and to use the trophy fee to buy a couple of young female rhinos for further breeding and freshening up the bloodstock.

We stood looking at the pile, or midden, of freshly steaming dung. The bull rhino is territorial, and this is its way of marking territory. Middens serve both as optical and olfactory signs. The rhino defecates and urinates and then scuffs the dung around with its feet and horn to enhance the wall of smell. Judging by the size of this one, it had been used for years. Other rhinos had added to the latrine, no doubt, which was now crawling with dung beetles.

Swarms of flies also droned and buzzed slowly above the midden as if drugged by the thick, scent-laden air. Nearby there was a broken tree stump, polished to a high shine by rhinos rubbing up against it. Rhinos have a heavy load of ectoparasites such as ticks and lice. They can remove some of these by wallowing in mud and then letting the mud dry, thus entombing the pests. A rub on a tree stump will usually dislodge them, whilst giving a glossy finish to the stump. Also, the mud cools the rhino and protects its skin from the sun and further pest infestations.

Leading off the midden was the characteristic three-toed spoor of the bull. It was easy to see in the fine sand. It had become a familiar sight to us as we had tracked it over the passage of several days. The summer had been good, and the abundant rain had made the bushveld a green curtain behind which everything could hide, including three tonnes, and more, of rhino. The wind had turned into a capricious whore. She flirted with us, gently kissing the back of our necks, then blowing false promises into either ear, before breathing in our faces. This was not conducive to tracking an animal possessing an excellent sense of smell, and we had been cuckolded enough earlier. The rhino had picked up our scent and, although we hadn't seen it, we had heard it crash through the bushes. The spoor had led us to the midden. After excreting an immense pile of sloppy green dung, the rhino had left. We took up the spoor again.

The rhino was in no hurry and had stopped to crop the grass. Our black tracker, Thomas, was certain that we were no more than half an hour behind the quarry. The bushes crowded in on us from all sides. We started to move in on the rhino.

The rhino now stood dozing about fifty metres before us. The wind was good for the moment, but the rhino was not standing broadside. The cover here was now sparser, but, as rhinos can't see well, we dared to move in. The sound of a twig breaking underfoot reached it, and it turned to peer myopically in our direction. It sniffed but could not detect any taint of our scent. The big trumpet ears flicked erratically. The rhino snorted and swung around and turned to face us full on. It knew that we were there. I knew then that the rhino would charge. Would this be the place where something would die? The front brain shot was the only chance from this angle. I raised my rifle and put off the safety and brought the cross hairs of the scope to where they should be. The electric tension was discharged as the rhino uttered a short snuffling grunt, turned again, and pounded away into the bush. The rush of adrenaline made us light headed as we unwound from the close shave.

"That was as near as *damn it* is to swearing," I said, putting on the safety again and turning to my friends.

They both grinned, trying unsuccessfully to cover their fear.

"I thought that you would have to shoot. The old boy seemed to toss a mental coin, and it must have come up heads, meaning that he chose to tail it," replied my PH, putting his rifle into a safe condition in one easy action.

"I'll drink to that," I said, wiping the sweat off my brow.

We unwound, drank hot water out of the bottles, and set off again. The paths were covered with rhino spoor, and it was difficult to sort out the spurious tracks. We pressed onward. An hour later we had closed to the last thirty metres. We could make out the head of the rhino as it stood under a tree. The bush throbbed with the sound of insects. We closed in. Sweat stung my eyes as if chili extract were being poured over them. The strident chirping of the insects augmented the roar of blood in my ears as I raised the rifle to shoot. The rhino was standing broadside, and I placed the cross hairs on the place. Hey! Wait a minute. This was not the same rhino. I looked at the tracker near me. He shrugged his shoulders and signaled to me not to shoot. I didn't.

My blood was pumping around so fast that I feared the rhino would hear the swish of it surging around inside me. We had picked up the spoor of another bull. It was not so big in the horn department as the one we wanted. It was also younger and therefore definitely off the wanted list. We retraced our footsteps, carefully avoiding the treacherous wait-a-bit thorns while trying to keep our eyes on the rhino. The rhino swung around to face us. It snorted. Oh, oh, this was going to be it. I saw it all in my mind's eye, trying to explain to the landowner how we had ended up with the wrong rhino. The rhino stood peering around, radar-dish ears flicking this way and that, trying to detect sound. It took a half pace forward, appeared to make a decision, blew air through its nostrils, and turned and stormed off, crashing through bushes it mowed down before it. Another close shave.

Rifles were uncocked and nerves unwound. Rhino hunting is not good for your nervous system, and adrenaline depletion can be a real problem. Those who have seen rhino in the zoo, walled off by a substantial barrier, have no idea how big they look when they are right up in front of you, with no protection between you and oblivion. We called it a day, having had enough fun and games with rhinos for the time being.

That night, after a meal of grilled impala liver and kidneys and after a corresponding nightcap of several stiff tots of something tawny brown that burned like fire as it descended, I fell into bed and then into a weird tumbling condition, in that order.

"Come on; get up! We've got a rhino to hunt!"

The voice of my PH penetrated the Scottish mists of sleep, and I started to grunt and mumble the speech of the hung over and rudely awakened. Whisky poisoning, again. I dragged myself out of my bed and noticed that it had the appearance of a load of blankets spewed from a washing machine gone berserk. I made a dull mental note never, in the future, to chase down wine with anything other than wine.

In case you are wondering, no, we didn't get around to taking that rhino. We tracked and walked and talked and cursed and were bitten by flies, bugs, and ticks (but not snakes). We were scratched to bits by wait-a-bit thorns (but not cats), and the blisters on our feet burned in our boots as if we had pulled on socks made of glowing coals. We did everything. It wasn't enough. We did that extra bit. Still no luck. Maybe one day I'll go back and go through the whole process again. Close shaves, you see, can be addictive.

Chapter 6

Hippopotamus

(*Hippopotamus amphibius*)

The hippopotamus, or hippo, meaning "river horse," was once widely distributed throughout Africa where sufficient water was available. It was just as common a sight on the Nile as it was in Cape Town. It still is a fairly common animal, and contact with humans increases as the plantations of sweet potato, mango, millet, cabbage, and watermelon encroach the riverbanks. An adult bull hippo will weigh up to three tonnes, reach a metre and a half at the shoulder, and attain a length of over three metres. The cows are smaller. Mating and birth, some eight months later, takes place in the water. Hippos may attain fifty years in age.

The hippo can remain immersed for up to five minutes before coming up for air. Both sexes are capable of opening their jaws to a wide angle and know how to use their long, ivory teeth. The hippo is a vegetarian, despite having teeth seemingly more suited to a sabre-toothed tiger. Most of the time the hippo lies in the water, which helps support its considerable weight. Also, the water protects its naked skin from the heat of the sun. As dusk comes, hippos leave the water to feed on all types of vegetation and to wreak havoc in native plantations. For this reason they are hunted. Hippos can run quickly despite their bulk and have a short temper, and it is due to this that hippos are responsible for many attacks on humans. For that deadly reason, too, they are hunted. The hippo is one horse that I'd bet odds on to cause trouble, one way or another.

Hunting the Hippo: Never Look into the Mouth of This Horse

The black woman had been visiting a neighbouring village and had left, for her appointment with death, later than intended. The thick and tart native beer that she'd consumed in considerable quantities had been good. She had started on her journey home just as the sun slid away in the west. The full moon that came up to replace it was a cold disk beaming its silvery light onto the bushveld. She had taken this riverside path many times before, and it was easy to follow the river downstream for a few kilometres. She reckoned that, even in her advanced state of inebriation, she would be home within a couple of hours. She belched appreciatively and continued.

When she had been a girl, fifty years earlier, the area had been dangerous because of the lions and crocodiles. Now, with the encroachment of civilization and the erection of game fences by the farmers, there was really nothing to worry about, except, perhaps, for the odd snake. The *nogas* were the only things that worried her, as they were harbingers, mostly of death. The bite of the black mamba was a quick nerve-poison death; the puff adder's bite was a slow, agonizing death from the poisoning of tissue and blood.

Alongside the path, the villagers had planted their crops in the fertile soil of the riverbank. The abundance of water and the sweet richness of the black soil made it possible to reap a good harvest of millet, cabbages, and potatoes. Such abundance had also attracted animals partial to the succulent vegetables. The woman continued on her way, and the ivory-filled jaws got closer with every step she took.

She was near to home, now, but death was also much nearer. She did not yet feel the danger as she stooped to relieve herself. It was only when she straightened up that she sensed menace behind her. At first she discounted the sensation as the effects of the beer. She sniffed loudly and spat a stream of dark tobacco juice out the side of her mouth.

She continued on, but her misgivings gave way to terror as she felt the earth tremble and heard the rumble bearing down on her. She turned and saw the immense bulk of the moon-washed gray black beast. Her legs went weak and wobbly as the claws of fear clutched at her and held her fast. She tried to run, but the bull hippo caught her. Just as it reached the woman, it swung its massive head to the side and opened its mouth to expose the great arcs of ivory there. The tusks, stained brown from vegetable juice and honed to razor sharpness by rubbing against each other, glinted dully in the moonlight for a split second. Then they vanished with a dull crushing sound as they scythed deeply into the woman.

Her shrill scream ended abruptly as the hippo harvested her as if mowing grass. The unstoppable momentum of the attack catapulted her forward, and the *kubu* shook its head, worrying her the way a terrier shakes a rat. The sharp ivory scissors snipped wickedly through meat, nerves, tendons, and organs as neatly as a surgeon's scalpel. Intense, sudden shock and loss of blood from her punctured lungs, liver, and intestines caused her to sink into merciful unconsciousness. Merciful because she would not feel the bone-pulverizing weight of the feet of two thousand kilograms of hippo as it finished its deadly work by stamping her into the mud of the riverbank. Satisfied that the intruder in its territory was dead, the river horse trotted back to the cabbage patch it had been raiding.

Hyenas came later that night. The *mpisi*, giggling hysterically at the joke of the woman's bad fortune and their own good luck, finished off the meat. They left only a few chewed bones, a bloody smear on the soil, and a few shreds of clothing in the wake of their feast.

Dawn came and the sky streaked red. The doves stared down from their leafy perches onto the shreds of death and started up their mournful, questioning calls of *who, who, whooo, whoo who.* The great hippo went down the riverbank on its usual path as though nothing had happened and sank quietly into the river. In Africa, certain rivers may be calm, but they are never empty.

I had zeroed in the rifle, calibre .375 H&H Magnum, precisely, using 300-grain full-metal-jacket bullets. This precision calibration is necessary because the only viable shot on a hippo in the water is the brain shot. Brain shots require precision placement, and the bullet must be able to penetrate the massive bone surrounding the brain. For such penetration, it is essential that the bullet does not deform or disintegrate; a full-metal-jacket bullet consists of a hardened lead core (for weight) surrounded and bonded into a steel case. One can also use solid bullets that are a piece of tough copper alloy, also characterized by a tendency to deform only slightly upon contact.

The brain shot (which means hitting a small and difficult target) is best because a hippo is capable of creating much havoc and damage before succumbing to a shot in the heart-lung area. Also, hippos are in water the majority of the time and expose only the very top of their heads. Hippos leave the water at night and may be taken on their exit or entry paths, but the question remains about whether there will be sufficient light to shoot straight. Artificial lighting is illegal in most places. Any boat venturing near a breeding herd of hippos is a candidate for a capsize, because lovesick hippos are cantankerous. In love or not, they are vicious. A wounded hippo is an extremely dangerous adversary, capable of smashing a boat in two and turning the unfortunates inside into instant crocodile fodder. Their extreme aggressiveness, wounded or not, is probably due to their strong sense of territory. Bulls in a mating mood fight viciously for the favours of a female. Except when they come out of the water at night to feed, hippos pass the day away in various states of immersion.

There are two tactics used for hunting hippo. The first requires that the hunter find the main tracks used by the hippo to exit and enter the water. These are large paths devoid of vegetation. The hunter waits nearby in the early evening or morning and can shoot the hippo as it leaves, or returns to, the water. Hippos have well-developed senses and can run fast. They can overtake a runner no matter what brand of pumps the unfortunate is wearing. The hunter must therefore make the first shot count and hit the brain. Such an injury will cause the hippo to drop on the spot. A second insurance shot, in the shoulder-heart-lungs area, may then be given. If the shot placement is not ideal, the hunter has a serious problem on his hands. As can be imagined, hippos do not take kindly to having lumps of steel and lead bounced off the top of their skulls at high velocity. It is here that the "backup rifle" of the PH comes in handy. A PH usually carries a larger calibre rifle than his client and in such cases can stop the hippo (or any other game) with a bullet in the right place.

The second way to hunt hippo is to stalk the animal, either from the riverbank or in a boat. Some may say that this is not sporting since the hippo is in the water. That may be the case under normal circumstances, but when a rogue animal is being culled, the object is to remove it, quickly and efficiently, with the least element of danger. No hunter wants to die stalking big game, any more than racing car drivers, glider pilots, or in-line skaters do exercising their sports. Sure, the excitement of the possibility of an accident is there, but the crux of the matter is in putting your skill to the test. If Lady Luck is with you, your skill will prevail. You will live to hunt (or drive or fly or skate) another day.

The stalk-from-the-riverbank method has the advantage that the hunter has a steady support for the rifle, and that is conducive to accurate bullet placement; a rocking boat is not. Also, hippos will see an approaching boat and may become restless. The bulls may even attack it, believing it to be another bull encroaching on their territory.

Assuming you do shoot well and hit the brain, the hippo will sink immediately, floating to the surface only when the stomach contents have fermented enough to generate buoyant gases that will bring the carcass to the surface. This process usually takes about two or three hours, depending on the hippo's stomach contents and the water temperature. This method is avoided when there is a strong river current present or if there are crocodiles around. Once afloat, the bloated hippo is towed to the riverbank and skinned out there. A very close watch must be kept for suspicious-looking "logs" that float against the current and get slowly nearer the workplace. Crocodiles have a good sense of smell and will pick up the taint of blood in the water from quite a distance.

After a long and dusty journey, my PH and I arrived at the village, Tonga Block B, on the Swaziland border. We met the authorities and the local chief, or *induna*. After hearing out Chief Benjamin, who recounted the long list of heinous demeanours accredited to the hippo, now peacefully resting in the river, we set off to cull it. Unfortunately, word had got out about the forthcoming demise of the hippo, and a couple thousand spectators had already assembled along the riverbank. They were eager to see the end of their troubles and to secure a piece of free meat when all was done. Meat is a prized commodity in protein-starved Africa. The natives were in a hippo hysteria, and much ribaldry was going on among the youths. One enterprising old crone had even set up a makeshift stall under an umbrella and was doing a brisk trade selling homemade beer that she offered from a cracked green plastic cup. Once drained, it was returned, refilled, and passed straight on, without being washed, to the next customer. Looking at the mass of chanting black humanity assembled there, I could imagine how those at Rorke's Drift in Natal Province, South Africa, on 22–23 January 1879, during the Zulu wars, must have felt. We didn't know it at the time, but history was about to repeat itself. Ah well, off to work.

The bank sloped down steeply toward the river, which flowed with a barely perceptible current. In the middle of the river was a sandbar that broke the surface like the dorsal fin of a shark. Next to it, the hippo stood in the water with only its nostrils, pig-pink eyes, and tiny flicking ears visible. It submerged for a couple of minutes at a time, giving us the chance to approach. We got to a place nearly opposite the beast and surveyed the situation through binoculars. The hippo was taking no notice of the commotion caused by the people on the banks high above. The number of spectators grew every minute as contingents from outlying villages arrived. The hippo had not changed position for the last five minutes, so I lay down and rested the rifle across my rolled-up pullover for support and sought the hippo through the telescopic sight.

I chambered a bullet and waited. I judged the distance to be about eighty metres. I estimated that the bullet would strike at a speed of about seven hundred metres per second and yield four and a half thousand joules of energy. To give an idea of such energy, one must imagine a mass of five hundred kilograms (half a metric tonne) being dropped from a height of one meter. That's roughly the impact of the bullet: fairly powerful stuff. The resulting "headache" would be fatal. Since the bullet would be traveling at more than twice the speed of sound, it would get to the hippo before the report of the rifle fire. In other words, if the shot placement was exact, the hippo would never hear it.

The hippo surfaced, spraying water droplets from its nostrils like a shower of diamonds that sparkled in the sunlight. I brought the cross hairs of the telescopic sight midway between the bulbous eye and the ear, and an inch or so low. I never felt the kick of the rifle, but I did hear the whiplash crack of the bullet's impact on the hippo's bony head a fraction of a second after the bullet was fired. A great sigh erupted from the spectators as the hippo slid out of sight. It made a *plop-swish* sound as the water foamed over it in a plume of spray. I chambered another bullet and waited.

After five minutes there was still no sign of the hippo, and we began to relax. Suddenly, a great cry pierced the air as the spectators saw the patch of blood that was now slowly spreading in the water, colouring it rusty red. Soon all the people were shrilling at the top of their voices, and then pandemonium broke loose as they poured toward the river's edge. Several of them lost their footing. They were ignored and trampled. The driving force behind all this was their application of logic: One rogue hippo, now clearly dead, equals plenty of prime meat up for grabs. However, they had not reckoned that the hippo was down and under and was going to remain as such for at least two hours. The crowd stood in consternation when told that the hippo was not ready to come out of the water just yet.

Their mood became sullen and ugly. The induna was told that the dead hippo had first to float to the surface before the crowd could get their meat. He understood this. He then made a long speech using much gesticulation and pointing, with a small club he carried in his hand, first to the hippo blood and then to my rifle. The people listened but were not happy. After all, they had seen the white men come with rifles and had seen the hippo's blood. According to African logic, that meant meat and lumps of succulent fat, so where was it? They wanted the meat, now.

We managed to push our way from the river's edge and through the menacing press of the crowd. The atmosphere seemed to buzz from the electricity of the situation. We knew that it needed only slight provocation to precipitate a fight between rival bands jealous to get their share of the meat. Furthermore, it was clear that we would become mixed up in the whole affair.

Miracles do happen, because we got back to the Jeep. We had left someone near the river to observe the situation, and, above all, the behaviour of the crowd. Three hours later, when the sun was well down in the western sky, we heard a cry from the crowd and, at the same time, the walkie-talkie crackled with the news: The hippo had surfaced.

When we got to the riverbank, we saw the beast floating in the same spot where it had slid from view. It was like a great gray barrage balloon, bobbing gently in the water. An inflatable outboard motorboat was launched, and we went across to the hippo. We had our rifles, and I had removed the telescopic sight to enable me to get off a quick shot should it be necessary; one can never be sure of any animal in this situation. The old saying "It's the dead ones that get up and kill you" is a good one to remember.

This hippo was in no position to get up and kill anybody anymore. We threw a thick rope around its stubby hind leg. The tow back toward the riverbank went easily, but then we came to a soggy halt as the hippo ploughed into the soft mud about two metres from the bank. The natives had been watching the progress. When they had verified that the hippo presented no danger to them, they swarmed over the carcass. They started jabbing it with sticks and trying to slash it with all manner of sharpened instruments. Several natives screamed and staggered backward, clutching deeply cut arms and lacerated hands, injuries inflicted by overenthusiastic butchers already at work. The injured ones didn't take too kindly to this random mutilation of their bodies, and violent fights broke out in the ranks as friends and relatives swarmed to help the injured and to take sides. It was hell.

Chief Benjamin and his bodyguards managed to subdue the various combatants by swinging rapid and accurate blows at their woolly skulls and shiny pates with evil-looking knobbed wooden clubs. Judging by the sharp click the clubs made upon contact with a cranium, it was a wonder that nobody was killed outright with a crushed brain. After law and order had been reestablished, we could continue to remove the hippo from the water. Using a combination of human muscle (the natives were now eager to help), a four-wheel-drive Jeep, ropes, a powerful electric winch, and plenty of cussing, we succeeded. It seems to me that there is nothing quite as heavy as a dead hippo. The corpulent beast was a very dead weight, and soon the natives were sweating and glistening like anthracite coal as they toiled to drag their meat away from the river. By the time two tonnes of hippo was on land, night had come.

We forced the great jaws open and saw, in the torchlight, the length of the razor-edged tusks. It is amazing that, despite having teeth to make any carnivore green with envy, the hippo is a pure vegetarian. The dark brown, stained tusks had deep longitudinal grooves in them. The working surfaces were a rich honey yellow and polished as smooth as a billiard ball. We removed the head for a shoulder mount and some of the hide to make into leather, and all the time the natives were pressing closer and chanting. Some of them had already gouged chunks from the carcass and had eaten the gory meat raw. Then it became impossible to hold them back, and they swarmed over the hippo like ants. We dragged the trophy away and stood back, happy to be out of the chaos. We heaved the skull and skin onto the Jeep and drove away into the night, leaving the natives to their butchery.

The following day we skinned the hippo skull out and salted the skin. It would make excellent leather, when planed down and tanned. A close inspection of the skull revealed that the shot had been exactly on the button. The bullet had exited on the other side after passing directly through the centre of the brain cavity. We also saw something that we hadn't seen the night before: a scrap of native cotton cloth that was jammed solidly between two molars. The killer river horse was no more.

The Cape buffalo bull sang its death bellow before dying in this thick mopane bush. RSA.

The leopard was a big tom. Here he is showing you the size of his paws, which are loaded with butter-yellow claws, covered with a film of rotting meat. Hoedspruit region, Mpumalanga, RSA.

After we got him cleaned up, he agreed to have his photo taken (I mean the author!) RSA.

Black trackers are indispensable for finding game and following up blood spoor. They have phenomenal eyes and courage. They also have an unshakable belief in the shooting abilities of the hunter. RSA.

A leopard took this blesbok up into a tree and wedged it in the branches. Leopards do this to prevent lions, hyenas, or any other animal from stealing their share. After eating about half, it left the rest to ripen. Hoedspruit region, Mpumalanga, RSA.

A couple of young bull elephants take a welcome drink from one of the many artificial water troughs. Game management programs provide water to reduce loss of wildlife. Hoedspruit area, Mpumalanga, RSA.

Elephants are so big you can't see them. We stalked up to this one with the camera. RSA.

I dropped this bull instantly with the side brain shot using a .375 H&H Magnum, 300 grain, full-metal jacket. Shooting from a distance of twenty-eight metres, there was no room for error. RSA.

Shame on me! If you look closely, you will see that I got scoped! RSA.

The butchery team at work. Nothing goes to waste in game management. The elephant meat was destined for sale to the locals. RSA.

This young elephant bull followed our Jeep for some time. Under such circumstances, you should never switch off your vehicle's engine. RSA.

That winter the bush was thick and this five-year-old lion blends into the dry leaves. Although one needs to be cautious when taking close-up pictures, this lion was quite obliging. Hoedspruit area, Mpumalanga, RSA.

The lioness looks almost friendly, but I was glad to be atop the Jeep. RSA.

Lions are either sleeping or eating. This lioness has just awakened and is having a quick snack on a piece of very ripe meat. RSA.

Left: Lions in the bushveld normally don't have great manes. As you can see, this was a big male—just goes to show what eating Cape buffalo can do for you. I had a rug made of this one, and my dogs still won't get near it! RSA.

Lioness in the mopane bushes. This one snarled at us but didn't attack. The trouble with lions is that they are unpredictable. Always exercise caution. RSA.

They're normally not dangerous, but when you are twenty metres away armed with only a camera, white rhino do not look that docile. RSA. (Safari Press photo library)

After the shot, we went out to see if the hippo was lying in shallow water. It wasn't. The murky depths would yield up the hippo only some hours afterward when the fermenting stomach contents had produced sufficient gas. RSA.

Left to right: Helper, yours truly, and Chief Benjamin of Tonga Block B. Don't let this serene moment fool you; a serious crowd-control problem developed when the hippo meat hit the riverbank. RSA.

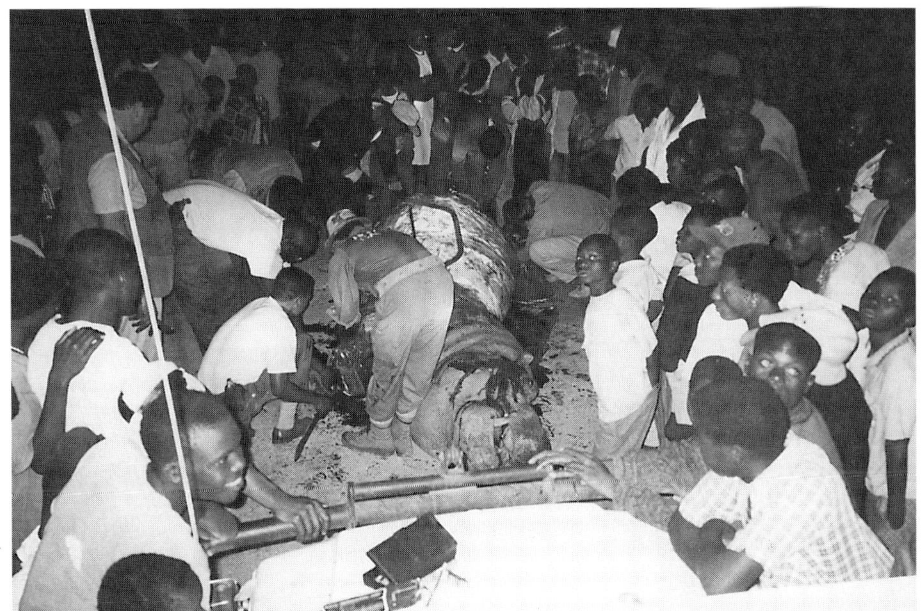

The (overly) enthusiastic butchers of Tonga Block B surround the hippo. It was at precisely this time when things got out of hand. It was like Rorke's Drift, again. RSA.

A nice bushbuck, taken after years of waiting for Lady Luck to smile; however, I jabbed my thumb with the tip of a horn. That injury was to develop into a nice breeding place for African bacteria. RSA.

The oryx, or gemsbok, of Namibia is tough to bag. The bulls have shorter but thicker horns than the cows. No matter, either sex can skewer you into a very passable kabob. Namibia.

A trophy impala taken with the .375 H&H Magnum. The Silvertip bullet entered the chest, dropping the old ram on the spot. RSA.

The baboon was a big male. The size of its teeth should convince you that baboons can be as dangerous as any leopard. In fact, leopards are regularly attacked and "seen off the premises" by packs of baboons. RSA.

This impala went a long way before we could get it. It's hard to say whether the bullet or the black mamba killed it. RSA.

If you look closely at this baboon, you will see its swollen jaw and lower lip. The baboon must have been in great pain. It's face was full of pus, and it stank of the corruption raging in its flesh. RSA.

The red hartebeest is an attractive game animal. No other species has such thick curled-up-and-back horns. RSA.

Blue wildebeest, together with their black wildebeest cousins, are considered the clowns of the African bushveld. They are always alerting other animals to the presence of hunters with their snorting and prancing antics! RSA.

The gray duiker is a common animal with uncommon habits for it will occasionally eat meat. Hunting this quick gray shape in the bush is a great challenge. I wasn't even hunting duiker when this one made an error. The measurement tape put him well into the Rowland Ward book. One up to me, Mr. Murphy! RSA.

Lions had pulled off a strip of this trophy blue wildebeest bull's skin, leaving such a mess that we didn't even bother to take a photo of that side. This wildebeest took my Silvertip in .375 H&H Magnum in the front of the chest. RSA.

After shooting this wildebeest, I discovered that one of the bull's hind legs was broken and swollen with infection. A long and painful death is usually the fate of injured animals, although lions and hyenas help out if they can. RSA.

Chapter 7

Hunting Plains Game

The Big Five animals are the elephant, rhino, Cape buffalo, lion, and leopard. Hippo and giraffe are also big but do not have membership cards for the Big Five club. Pity. They could all be put together and called the Magnificent Seven. Do not despair. There are many other game species that may not be as big or imposing or even as dangerous, but their observation and hunting can be just as much of a challenge. These are called the plains game—not because they are a lacklustre lot but mostly because of where they live. The daily PH fee is lower for them than when a Big Five animal is being hunted, and many hunters start with plains game animals to gain experience.

The idea about an animal's being big making it dangerous is only relative. It's irrelevant whether a bushbuck's horn or an elephant's tusk is stabbed through your chest; they will have exactly the same effect on your retirement plans. Many people, for example, have suffered from "bushbuck poisoning" of one form or another. On one occasion I received my own overdose of bushbuck.

Bushbuck
(*Tragelaphus scriptus*)

The bushbuck, or poor man's kudu (it's related), has notched up quite a few injuries and deaths on its needle-sharp spiral horns. This small antelope is a prized trophy, as it is secretive, alert, and quick. It is usually seen only very early in the morning, just as the night gives way to dawn, or in the evening when the dusk turns to night. In South Africa, this means that you have about half an hour in the morning or evening to get lucky. For that reason, it is a very challenging hunt.

The bushbuck reaches about one and a half metres in length and stands just over a metre at the shoulder. A mature buck will tip the scales at about sixty kilograms. The bushbuck has a rich, dark-brown coat dappled with white spots. Its face is also marked with white spots, and its head is topped off with long spiraled and pointed horns that exceed twenty-five centimetres in old bucks. It knows how to use those horns too, and will attack with deadly determination if cornered. Many a predator has paid for its folly in getting near to a wounded bushbuck; many a hunter has been surprised by the lightning penetration of its horns through clothing and into the body. The bushbuck is never found far from water and has a fixed territory that it guards against other males. The bushbuck is dangerous, dead or alive.

Hunting the Bushbuck: Trouble with Horns

It was August. We were near to Hoedspruit in Mpumalanga, South Africa, and had filled our hunting bag, except for bushbuck. I had often hunted for the common bushbuck but was becoming convinced that it was incorrectly named, for I had rarely seen it. Friends of mine, however, always had success. It riled me to hear how they were able to get out of the Jeep, in full daylight, walk to the next convenient tree, rest their rifle on it, and shoot. A check with the tape measure and yet another entry into Rowland Ward's book would follow. Whenever I visited, the results of my friends' bushbuck-hunting success would stare down at me with mocking, glassy-eyed expressions from lofty positions on trophy room walls. With time I became disillusioned and told myself, *Who wants a damn bushbuck, anyway?* and had gone off hunting other beasts. Don't tell anyone, though, but I still kept an eye open for a "bushy," just in case. It became a jinx, for I could never get Lady Luck to conspire with me to obtain a bushbuck for my trophy room.

It was a week before my last hunt of the year and we had been in an area where, it was reputed, there was a good male bushbuck. We had found sign of bushbuck presence in the form of droppings, and had even been treated to a fleeting glimpse of a Mister Bushbuck's missis. Of the old gentleman, though, we saw not a hair. Now, at the end, I had resigned myself to departing with no bushbuck; I told myself, again, "Who wants one, anyway?"

We had set off earlier than usual this morning and were hunting warthog for the pot. The traditional South African *potje* is a wonderful way to prepare game meat over a fire in a pot like a miniature cauldron. If tough meat from an old animal becomes as tender as veal, just imagine the results when you start off with tender meat. Warthogs, one of which would suit our potje nicely, are active by day. When evening comes they return to their holes in the ground. Knowing where a band of warthogs had their hole and that they would leave when dawn arrived, we decided to ambush them as they left their premises and reduce their number by one.

It was still dark when we left the Jeep, about two kilometres away from the warthog hole. A tracker called Winston led, my PH was second, and I brought up the rear. We got into position behind a boulder about sixty metres from the warthog's hole and waited. I put my binoculars on the black entrance to the hole, hoping to detect a movement as the warthogs left. It was too early, though, and I couldn't see a thing.

The dawn came slowly, and by 5:45 A.M. the light was sufficient to make out some details; in another quarter of an hour it would be shooting light. By 6:15 A.M. there had still been no movement from the warthogs' hole. Maybe they were having a lie-in or had moved residence without telling us. The sun steadily warmed the chill off the air and the louries, or "go-away birds," were weakly fluttering about in the trees and bushes, telling us to do just that. The louries are the bane of the hunter, for the blasted birds fly up in front, warning everything of your presence with their nasal-toned *Go 'way, go 'way!* They are parrot-beaked and monotone in colour, being a bluish ashy gray. Even their filigree cockatoolike headcrest, which they raise continually, is gray.

There was a movement in front of the warthogs' hole as a mongoose went by. I watched this archenemy of snakes go about its business. The mongoose is not immune to the bite of venomous snakes, as is popularly believed. Fatalities are rare, however, because of the unbelievably rapid reactions of which the animal is capable. High-speed filming reveals that a snake's strike goes mostly into the empty space where there had been a mongoose standing, one hundredth of a second before. The mongoose paused for a moment at an interesting stone. It lifted a front paw like a dog pointing a pheasant. A second later it delved under the stone with such a rapid scratching action that its paws became a blur and something was converted into breakfast. We could hear the smacking of the mongoose's mouth as it devoured the delicacy with obvious relish. I only ever found snails, slugs, worms, snakes, centipedes, millipedes, woodlice, and scorpions under stones. I could therefore speculate on what the mongoose had found. A moment later the mongoose scurried off quickly into the undergrowth. Maybe it went to get some antacid tablets.

If the warthogs had intended coming out today, they were late. I glanced at my watch: already 7 A.M. So much for getting up extra early and executing the great warthog ambush plan. However, hunting is like this; you never, ever, can be sure of anything. I felt a slight poke in the ribs. The perpetuator of this universal sign of "Watch out, something is coming" was Winston. He moved his head slightly to the left and pointed slowly to the biggest bushbuck I had ever seen in my life (not that I'd seen many, up till then). The buck was about sixty metres away, broadside to me, and moving between the scrub toward the thick green riverbank reeds. After all, it was late for any self-respecting bushbuck to be out. My PH was already nodding his approval and my rifle went up. The cross hairs of the telescopic sight were quickly brought onto the bushbuck's shoulder. The distance had now increased to about eighty metres, and the bushbuck showed no indication at all of stopping to let me shoot him. A sharp whistle from my PH surprised the bushbuck more than it did me, and the buck stopped dead to see what had caused the noise. It remained dead. In its tracks. At the shot, the gang of warthogs, squealing porcine abuse at us, poured forth from the hole and vanished into the bush. They had known that we were waiting for them and had been too scared to come out. The noise of the rifle fire had broken their nerve, and they had left, head over trotter. With dismay, we saw our pork chops vanish into the maw of the bush. However, we guessed that bushbuck filets, accompanied by a suitable wine, would taste just as good, if not better.

We went up to where the buck had fallen and saw the blood trail leading off into the reeds. The buck had got to its feet whilst we had been diverted, momentarily, by the warthogs. The blood on the spoor was bright pink and foamy, indicating a lung shot. We went farther forward and found the bushbuck lying on a carpet of blood. I went up to it, rifle scope removed and ready to fire another shot if necessary.

It wasn't. I stooped down and caught hold of one of the twisted horns, tipped with needle-sharp points. As I did so, the bushbuck underwent a severe jolt as its muscles contracted in death. My grip on the horn was not good, and it slipped out of my grasp. The needle-tipped horn drove deeply into the ball of my thumb. Blood welled up, and the application of a bandage didn't help much. The pulsing flow of blood wasn't to be stopped so easily, and it soaked straight through the bandage and dripped onto the ground.

We sent Winston back to get the Jeep. While he was away, we busied ourselves with the bushbuck and with bandaging my thumb. The Winchester .243-calibre bullet had penetrated the bushbuck's body diagonally and had exited after touching both lungs. That the animal could get up at all was surprising, but, then again, bushbucks are tough.

After taking its cape (the headskin and skull) for a headmount and loading the meat, I insisted that we have a cold beer to celebrate before going to the local doctor to get my thumb stitched up. When we did arrive at the doctor's, he prodded and poked the punctured region. He swabbed it out with a yellow liquid that looked like dog's urine and stunk like methylated turpentine. I don't know if such a concoction exists, but the description fits. It stung like aftershave on a face full of razor nicks. After putting in a few stitches, he bound up my thumb and sent me on my way with the well-used "It'll be all right in the morning." It wasn't.

That night we feasted, and the bushbuck filets lived up to expectations despite not having been hung to ripen. The Cape red wine was also excellent. I was glad that the warthogs hadn't been obliging, for, who knows, if they had exited on schedule the bushbuck would still be in the reeds and not in the salt, ready for shipment to the taxidermists. That's hunting for you. It's all to do with luck, chance, fate, coincidence, and being in the right (or wrong) place at a given time, depending on whether you are the hunter or the hunted. Draining the last glass of wine, we said our good-nights and struck the day from our total. Tomorrow would be the first day of the rest of our lives and, perhaps, the last day in the life of a game animal. It might also be the other way around. It nearly was.

During the early hours of the morning, a painful throbbing started up in my injured thumb. It was relentless and increased in pitch and intensity over the next hours. My thumb had become a breeding station for about a trillion bacteria. Within a day it was as red as a cherry and as painful as a ripe carbuncle. The next visit to the doctor entailed a lancing to let out the thick, yellow-as-custard pus. The antibiotic tablets I was given played hell with my digestive system. Despite all this, I lived. In retrospect, I suppose a bushbuck will get you with his horns one way or the other; this way was much less permanent than being skewered.

Greater Kudu (*Tragelaphus strepsiceros*)

In my opinion, the greater kudu is the most handsome antelope in Africa. With only a beige ground colour and just a few white pinstripes (like an anemic zebra), it can't compare to the rich, red-brown coat and white striping of the bongo, found in the jungles of central Africa. It cannot equal the rugged features of the gray waterbuck, with its long throat mane. It certainly doesn't have the wild and swept-back horns of the sable antelope, nor its rich blackish colour and white facial and belly markings. It doesn't even have the size of the Lord Derby eland or the smart, clean-cut features of the impala. Yet it has always held the undivided attention of hunters.

The greater kudu can leap more than two metres into the air from a standing start, but its most attractive attribute is its long, thick, and spiraled horns, ending in ivory-coloured tips. It is a large animal, and kudu meat is good and lean. A mature bull will weigh over three hundred kilograms and is about two and a half metres long and one and a half metres at the shoulder.

It likes the inaccessible parts of mountains. The kudu can climb anywhere and possesses excellent hearing and sense of smell, good eyesight, and a cautious nature that makes it a great sporting challenge. The trophy bulls are always alone, coming down from their lofty residences only in the mating season, May to July. Afterward, the very tired bulls are especially secretive and difficult to find. Believe me.

Hunting the Greater Kudu: Drive Yourself Mad in One Easy Lesson

The time was August, the season winter, and the land lay cold and brittle early each morning. The place was Omaruru, in Namibia, once called South-West Africa. In this part of the world, the arid climate has forged hardness and resilience into its flora and fauna. The lack of water and a sun that belts down heat through cloudless skies has created a dry land, but it is as rich as any tropical rain forest. The animals that live here are typified by the kudu, gemsbok (or oryx), steenbok, springbok, mountain zebra, leopard, cheetah, and warthog, not forgetting the baboons. In the northeast of the country, in the Caprivi Strip, elephants leave their spoor alongside that of lions.

We wanted an exceptional kudu, and that meant a horn length of at least fifty-eight inches, measured according to Rowland Ward's parameters. We already knew how difficult kudu hunting could be and were not under any illusions. We were aware of the fact that kudu is the antelope that has driven many hunters to near or total insanity. It was already driving us to the mental asylum: We had searched fruitlessly over an area covering some two hundred square kilometres and had found nothing. Females were everywhere, as well as the immature bulls with one or maybe two twists to their horns. They stared at us vapidly as we went past them.

A trophy bull has three twists to its horns. The best we ever saw was a bull with a tantalizing "two-and-a-bit" twists. He gave us a peek at his approximately fifty-three-inch horns for a few minutes before floating away into the thinner air of the mountains. That kudu just knew that we wouldn't shoot. I have also experienced this sort of behaviour with European animals. They recognize danger, and a hunter approaching without intent is assessed as such. The animal does not run far off. If you approach with a deadly serious intent and the animal sees you, it runs forever.

The days dragged on, and it became clear that the mature bulls had gone high up into the mountains. They probably wanted some peace from their womenfolk (can't blame them for that). My PH suggested that we drive to an outlying place, early in the morning, and sit and observe the area from an elevated position in the hope of spotting some kudu movement.

The next morning we sat kudu-spotting. With us were our two black helpers, who had the quaintly incongruous Germanic names of Herman and Klaus, reflecting the earlier influence of the German colony on this part of Africa. Both were excellent game spotters, trackers, and skinners. We had binoculars and they had nothing, but almost simultaneously, after about an hour, they both pointed far into the hazy, heat-shimmering distance and said those magic words: "Big kudu." But how big?

They explained to us, in meticulous detail, where the big bull with the long horns of many twists was. They were talking about a minute speck of gray standing by a grain of reddish rock about a light year away. The eyesight of these men was unbelievable. We questioned the trackers closely, for it seemed nigh impossible to see with the naked eye whether this touch of colour had a reasonable set of horns on it or not. You see, the average African is not so much interested in horns as in the share of meat that is forthcoming. We were assured, however, that the bull was *groot* ("great," as in large), and so we set off to have a short-range meeting with Mr. Big.

We shouldered our rifles and followed our trackers down into the valley and started going up the flank of the mountain on the other side, where our kudu was supposed to be. The going was difficult because of the myriad stones, which always seemed too big to climb over and yet too small to justify walking around. After this strenuous circumventing and climbing, interrupted now and then by a stop for a drink, our hearts were pounding madly. The sun had warmed away the chill of the morning and was now busily adding warmth to our already overheated and sweat-drenched bodies. Our thick coats and woolen jumpers were discarded layer by layer as we went forward.

About midday we stopped and looked back to where we had come from. The little rocky outcrop from which the kudu had been seen was now just a brown patch far away. Our trackers had gone ahead of us to reconnoitre, and we were glad for the respite and lay back wearily in the shade of a boulder. A quarter of an hour later they came back. They told us that the kudu had now moved down into a part of the valley that was like a wound slashed into the open flank of the mountain. The kudu had gone into the shade. This meant that we were above the animal, and a plan of approach was made. The geographical features made it necessary that we climb still higher; then, after about a mile or so, we could start the approach, moving downward at an oblique angle.

The wind was kind, and we made good progress. Way up on the top of a rocky outcrop a baboon barked a warning, and soon a whole troupe of them were screaming something not too complimentary at us. I hoped that the kudu would not take the baboons too seriously as I crawled the last three hundred metres on my stomach, following my PH and a tracker. Carefully, we came to the edge of the cliff that marked the side of the valley wall nearest to us. Now only the last few centimetres of crawling were left, and I checked that my rifle was ready and slowly elbowed myself to position. Raising my rifle while keeping as low as possible, I brought the telescopic sight up to my eye and eased forward the final centimetre to permit a view of the land (and my kudu) below.

Nothing. Nothing but rocks, scrub bushes, and sand. The kudu that had previously been resting under a camel-thorn tree was not there. It had obviously taken the screaming baboons very seriously indeed and had decided to evaporate to another place.

Yes, you read it correctly. "Evaporate" is the only word I can find to describe how a kudu can vanish. A kudu doesn't get big by being unreceptive to warnings concerning danger, either real or imagined. In this case, the baboons had warned it and every other thing around. Herman scrambled down to the place and inspected the spoor left on the parched ground. He took some dung left by the kudu and came back to us. The droppings were warm and moist and had been left some five to ten minutes earlier. We waited a quarter of an hour and then sent our trackers forward to see if they could spot our elusive pal with the gray suit and a sense of humour more twisted than its horns. They came back and told us the bad, but not unexpected, news: The kudu had gone up to the mountains again.

As we had much ground to cover and the shooting light would be gone in about two hours, we reluctantly decided to turn back and try the next day. We did, and we failed. We also failed the following day. We gave up on the last day of the hunt, just before rendering ourselves certifiable, ready to be carried away in straitjackets, foaming at the mouth, eyes popped out like organ stops, and legs twitching convulsively like swatted flies.

For all I know, that kudu is still up there in the mountains. I reckon that it will get so old that it will become senile and not bother to heed or even hear a baboon's warning one fine day. Then some hunter will be able to say later just how easy kudu hunting is!

Oryx
(*Oryx gazella*)

The oryx, or gemsbok, is one pile of a tough animal, and it could teach Cape buffaloes a few lessons about surviving in dry country and disregarding bullets. A mature bull will weigh up to two hundred kilograms and stand as much as a metre and a half high at the shoulder. The beige-gray, horse-sized oryx has a long, swishy tail and a horselike face, marked in black and white somewhat like that of a badger. Its head is adorned with a pair of metre-long black, rapier horns, lethal-pointed and ringed. The top thirds of the horns are not ringed, and so are better to jab and penetrate with. How useful. Females generally have longer horns but males have thicker ones. Whether the oryx is a male or female is a moot point, however, if you should find yourself, one unhappy day, nicely pierced through and doubling as a kebab for a cannibal. The oryx fears nothing and will turn and stick its horns into anything it feels is a threat. A wounded oryx regards everything as a threat and is as dangerous as any of the Big Five. In addition, the oryx shrugs off bullets like so many fleas, running a long way or, more likely, turning to attack. Anyone for kebabs?

Hunting the Oryx: Telescopic Trouble

I had been using my rifle in calibre .375 H&H Magnum a lot on this hunt. The day for departure was getting nearer, and I was running out of cartridges. I had already used up a full packet of twenty on target shooting alone. Constant checking of accuracy is essential throughout any hunt, and, anyway, I like target shooting. I had checked my rifle's performance the day before. The point of impact, with respect to the cross hairs, had moved higher and to the left.

I decided not to adjust for a few centimetres, since this fell into the normal scatter in practice. As I had only a few cartridges left, I didn't want to adjust the scope. That would have required further verification shots afterward. Mistake number one.

The Namibian sun this August day was like a splash of molten steel in the sapphire blue sky. It pelted heat down onto us, but, despite this, my PH and I were out hunting oryx near Omaruru. I had a permit for a bull oryx, and after three hours' stalking he was there, standing below us, about two hundred metres away. We had picked up the spoor earlier, leading from a nearly dried-out water hole that the oryx had visited during the night. We found that the droppings had become moister, and at one place the oryx had released a little urine that had still not been boiled off by the sun. Our little Bushman tracker tested the wind and waved to us to follow him as he scampered away, hard on the spoor. The terrain was a great sprawling mixture of rocky outcrops, tiny valleys, and small hills, and as we got to the top of a pile of rocks we saw the old oryx bull below us.

I lay down flat and brought the telescopic sight's cross hairs onto the shoulder of the oryx. I had to aim down at a fairly steep angle. Mistake number two. At the shot, the oryx tossed its head, stood where it was for a second, looked around, and then set off at a brisk trot. A follow-up shot raised a puff of dust, well behind its rear end. The oryx accelerated (can't blame him) and vanished. We waited a while and then went to the place where it had stood.

The Bushman called us over and pointed to a tiny mark in the sand: blood, but bad blood. Not pink, foamy lung blood or red organ blood but dark, almost black blood. From meat. The question of where I'd hit him was not clear from this picture. I had aimed on the shoulder, the distance was 180 metres, and the angle was down. That was it! I had forgotten to aim lower to compensate for the lessened pull of gravity, causing a high shot. Mountain high, valley low: Aim below. I had aimed as if the oryx had been straight in front of me, where the pull of gravity would have brought the bullet down to approximately the place at which I had aimed. However, the oryx had been standing steeply below me. The rifle was already shooting high, and then the error in aiming steeply downward had been added to that, giving a shot very high and to the left.

We left a piece of paper on the ground and went back to the place from which I had fired. I squeezed off a precious shot at the target. Our Bushman tracker, standing well off to the side, went and checked it: very high and missed by plenty was the verdict. So now we had a wounded oryx out there, and we still had no idea where the blood had come from.

We set off, following our Bushman. Every now and then he would stop and show a minute speck of blood or a bent twig and then continue. An hour had passed since my shot, and we had found no more blood for the last kilometre or so. Things were looking bad, and we knew we had to find the animal before the night came to seek out its prey. A wounded animal is a sure candidate for leopard, hyena, jackal, or anything else partial to meat. Our tracker still held the spoor, which was now invisible to me. In their minds these people become the animal they seek. They think like the wounded antelope, the stalking lion, or the scared impala.

We continued and then the Bushman stood still, pointing to a bush and indicating that the oryx was just on the other side. The distance was no more than fifty metres. The Bushman stepped aside; we walked on. Rifle at the ready, I eased forward step by half step and then saw the oryx. It was facing away at an angle. I raised the rifle, took aim low and to the right on the shoulder, and the oryx dropped. I put in a second shoulder shot for insurance.

We found only two holes, near to each other, on the shoulder. A small, dark smear of dried, crusty blood was visible on the neck. Tracing this upward, we found a hole that had been neatly punched out of the tip of its left ear, as one sees in farmyard cattle. My first shot had been one hell of a high one. Such a slight wound from an ear-piercing operation like this would never have been fatal. We tested the size of the hole in the pierced ear with my last, unfired bullet; it was a perfect fit.

Impala
(*Aepyceros melampus*)

The impala is a common antelope. It has a glossy reddish brown colour and is white underneath. It has dark bushes of hair on its rear feet that serve as scent spreaders. It adapts to many types of terrain and can live off meagre vegetation, since it can graze on grass and browse on shrubs. The rams can weigh up to sixty kilograms and be one metre at the shoulder. Dominant rams may accumulate a harem of forty or more ewes. One lamb is born about seven months after mating, and it can follow the ewe shortly after birth. The relatively thin, lyrelike horns are ringed and sweep out widely from the skull. Only the rams have horns. A ram's life is tough; with so many ewes to care for he is constantly fighting off younger rams who are trying to run off with his ladies.

Hunting the Impala: Long Shot Number One

The pizza-oven heat of the hour just after midday drew the water from our bodies the way blotting paper sucks up ink. Salt-rimmed tide marks were left on our shirt armpits and collars as we sweated our way to dehydration, and there was no wind to bring respite from the heat. Even the lizards had left their usual resting places on the rocks because of the intense heat. For them, it must have been like sitting on a pile of freshly spewed lava. If you wished, you could have cooked an egg on a boulder. Nevertheless, we were hunting for rations in the form of an impala ram on a concession north of Johannesburg, South Africa. The search for this particular impala was difficult because the terrain was open. Wind was absent but so was cover. Several times we had gotten to within range. Then, one or another of the impala's womenfolk (there were about twenty of them) would look up from grazing just at the critical moment. She would give a farting sound of warning, and we would be back to square one.

We were now on one side of an abandoned airstrip, the impalas were on the other, and a good three hundred metres separated us. That is a long distance for any rifle-bullet combination. Our ram was standing broadside to us, off to the right, keeping an eye on his ewes. I had the telescopic sight turned up to the maximum magnification, and the impala's image danced in the shimmering mirage air that washed and lapped above the ground like a lake of mercury. I supported the rifle on a set of homemade shooting sticks: three bamboo canes of equal length, held together near the top with a piece of inner tube. The makeshift tripod was a great help for stability but could do nothing to lessen the mirage effect. I held the cross hairs of the telescopic sight above the ram, about half its body depth over its shoulder. Not having to allow for lateral drift because of the absence of wind, I squeezed off the shot. The impala was already falling as the *dupf* sound of the bullet's impact came back to us.

We examined the ram. His graying muzzle and flanks were patterned with old scars as witnesses to a life spent fighting over females. Some healed scars were visible, whilst others had scar tissue upon which no more hair grew. The horns were battle-clashed and chipped, but the tips were still sharp enough to skewer anything to death. A look inside his mouth showed that his teeth were worn down to brown stubs. The bullet hole, low behind the shoulder, bubbled pink lung blood.

Later on, we measured the distance. At 340 metres the Silvertip bullet in calibre .375 H&H Magnum had fallen about 50 centimetres; it had been a long shot, all right.

Baboon (*Papio ursinus*)

Baboons are found almost everywhere in Africa. There are several species, but the present discourse is limited to the chacma baboon. The baboon has a strong hierarchy, led by a dominant male. All baboons are dangerous, but the males, for some reason called dogs, have big canine teeth that they can and do use at the slightest provocation. Peter Capstick has written with chilling reality about the killer baboons of Vlackfontein in his book *Death in a Lonely Land*. Whatever else you may do, do not underestimate baboons. They are apt to rearrange your features and are more than capable of killing you, given half a chance.

Baboons will eat just about anything in the insect, animal, and vegetable departments. They fear nothing, especially if they are far up on a cliff. The leopard relishes baboon meat, and it is thought that a leopard with experience hunting baboon can be dangerous to humans, since it appears to understand the anatomic similarities. I'm sure there's nothing personal!

Hunting the Baboon: Long Shot Number Two

I was called awake one morning by the urgent entreaties of my PH and David, our houseboy at the Vaalwater camp in South Africa, to come and shoot a baboon that was in his vegetable garden. I jumped out of bed and, still in my pyjamas, jammed on my glasses, snatched the .375 H&H from the rack, loaded it, and went out onto the verandah. The big dog baboon saw me and, stopping only to grab a handful of lettuce, scampered away, casting surly, menacing looks at us. We stood and watched it run down the large, open field.

Baboons had been causing much damage to crops and gardens alike and had been declared vermin, to be shot on sight. The crafty animals soon got the message that humans meant trouble and had learned to carry out their raids very early in the morning, when the "hairless monkeys" were still in bed. It is one thing to be able to hunt the destructive beasts and entirely another to shoot them. The baboons in this area had developed a taste for millet and maize, and had a sense for distance. They knew that, after about three hundred metres, there was no particular danger from humans or their rifles.

The lettuce thief stopped to have a snack way down in the field, reckoning that it was safe. It was unusual to see only one baboon, since they normally range about in family groups of up to forty. This old dog baboon was a displaced animal, in some way. I turned to David and shook my head.

"It's too far away. Pity."

David, who came from Malawi and spoke good but rather old-fashioned English, was not convinced.

"Sir, baboons cause me much distress and are a nuisance. They are filthy, vicious vermin and destroy my labours in the garden. They catch and kill the chickens and put so much fear into the survivors that they stop laying. The ones that do lay have their eggs stolen by the baboons. Baboons even steal food from the open kitchen window. They are copulating each day. Please, couldn't you try to shoot it? Maybe the sound of the shot will cause it to leave the premises, if nothing else."

I estimated that the baboon, which was now sitting on its backside, munching away at the lettuce, was at least three hundred metres away. I decided to try for the shot.

"All right, then, please go and get me a few thick cushions so that I can lay the rifle on them."

David returned with the cushions. I got the baboon into the telescopic sights, and when I had the cross hairs on its head, I squeezed off the shot. The bullet hit. The baboon jumped into the air, and it was over.

"*That* baboon is dead," David said with evident pleasure.

We stared out over the field at the crumpled thing lying there. I must confess that I felt sad, since the baboon had only been helping itself to a free meal. It didn't know that such actions were the stuff of which the death penalty was made.

We took our time to walk over to where it lay. The bullet had fallen because of the distance and had entered its chest. It had left an exit hole in its back. It bared its big, yellowed, canine teeth at us; they were mighty impressive, even in the rictus of death. Its face was swollen, and we became aware of an unpleasant smell. An infection had taken hold in a recent wound on the animal's cheek. The stink was terrible, and it was for this reason that it had been chased out of the family group and had been forced to go it alone. The stink might have attracted predators such as hyena or leopard. I didn't know of this affliction at the time I squeezed the trigger, but now I was glad that the animal was released from the corruption in its face. David was also glad, since there was now one less baboon to "copulate each day."

Red Hartebeest (*Alcelaphus buselaphus*)

The red hartebeest is an animal with an overly long face in black and brown. It has a thick pair of short, ringed horns that, after coming straight up out of the skull, bend back at approximately right angles to end in sharp points. The body is a rich, deep brown, and a good bull will weigh in at 150 kilograms and stand over one and a half metres at the shoulder. It is a typical plains game antelope, and its weirdly shaped horns, in the shape of a heart when viewed face on, make it an interesting trophy. All senses are highly developed in the red hartebeest, making it a challenge to hunt.

Hunting the Red Hartebeest: Trouble with Tracking

Three hours' car drive due north of Johannesburg in the Republic of South Africa brings you to a place called Vaalwater. Around this area are many farms and game reserves, where the animals that one can hunt include impala, eland, warthog, rhino, leopard, and many types of antelope, such as steenbok and red hartebeest. We were here to hunt the latter.

The spotting, stalking, and shooting had gone like clockwork. The red hartebeest had bounded off toward the left at the shot. The sound of the bullet strike had been music to our ears as we watched the animal vanish behind a rocky outcrop. We were amazed to see it bolt out from the other side as if the devil were biting its tail. It galloped away and into the thick yellow grass of the bush and was gone, leaving us only with the ringing of the rifle shot in our ears. I turned to my PH, who was staring into the distance.

"I know I've got it! The cross hairs of the scope were full on the shoulder as I squeezed off the shot. The distance was only about sixty metres; that's nothing for calibre .375."

"Yes," he replied. "I heard the bullet strike and saw the hartebeest almost fall down. Let's wait awhile and let him stiffen up. We'll then go to that outcrop there, where it bounded away, and pick up the spoor. It will be an easy and routine job to find it."

It was not.

With our Shangane tracker Andrees in front, we set off to find the red hartebeest. We picked up the fresh spoor a short distance from the outcrop but found no blood. Our tracker could easily follow the way the animal had taken, stopping now and then to point out a bent blade of grass, a snapped twig here and a freshly upturned stone there. He showed us scuff marks on the naked boulders where the hartebeest had passed and, farther on, a place where it had stopped and left a pile of droppings that looked like smooth, dull emeralds in the sunlight. He showed us where, another kilometre farther, the animal had stopped and chewed some foliage. He showed us everything possible except the one thing we needed to have: blood. Not one spot of the stuff was found on the spoor.

The sun now pounded us mercilessly, and we regretted that we had not taken anything along with us to drink, believing that we would soon find the red hartebeest. We turned back. Lizards like divas draped in sequined gowns nodded at us, as if agreeing with our decision, before scuttling away to the other side of the boulders they lay on. We now noticed the many cruel, needle-pointed grass seeds that had burrowed their way in through our socks and had started to perforate the sensitive skin on our sweat-basted, tired, and aching feet. You don't notice any of this when you are tracking and full with hope. Mind over matter, again. We picked our way back, making use of shadow to avoid the roasting heat of the sun. We went to where I'd taken the shot and stood looking at the marks in the sand where I had lain.

"This is the exact spot. The hartebeest was standing over there, and it cleared off toward that rocky outcrop to the left," I said, pointing to the place where our troubles for the day had started.

"Affirmative to all that," replied my PH. "But let's now go to the actual spot where you shot it and follow the spoor from there."

"All right, but since we saw the hartebeest exit from the other side of the outcrop, I don't think we can achieve much. We never found any blood farther up the trail, so I doubt that we will find any there."

We went to the place, and Andrees stooped down and picked up a few reddish-brown hairs. They were cut through cleanly, as if with a pair of scissors. A bullet traveling at more than two times the speed of sound may be better than either the Barber of Seville or Mr. Teazy Weazy, but I wouldn't recommend it. The spoor was clear and easy and went off to the left, as we had all seen. Andrees now picked out a tiny, ruby-red speck of blood on a grass stalk. It was cracked and dried by the heat, as it was now more than three hours since I had shot. Soon more blood appeared on the spoor. As we approached the rocky outcrop, the blood trail increased to the point that it appeared someone had poured the stuff out of a watering can. We rounded a corner and there before us lay a perfectly shoulder-shot and very dead hartebeest.

A reconstruction of the events led us to believe that there had been a second hartebeest hidden from our view, resting behind the rocky outcrop. It had bolted when the one I'd shot came in from one side. Mine had already fallen down dead as we watched the other animal bound away. We had fooled ourselves into believing that the animal that had run off was the shot one. All the time that we were tracking in the blistering heat, feeding ticks, and becoming scratched and skewered by all sorts of nasty plants—while chasing a perfectly healthy animal—mine was lying dead, not fifty metres from where it had been shot. What had appeared to be a routine, easy hunt had turned out to be a very arduous and vexing exercise, plagued with all the usual doubts of a bad shot or miss. This goes to illustrate that you can never be sure what will happen during a hunt. Ever.

Blue Wildebeest (*Connochaetes taurinus*)

Blue wildebeests, or brindled gnus, are probably one of the best known antelopes of Africa. The yearly migration of millions of these beasts has been well documented and filmed. Footage has been captured of crocodiles waiting patiently for the herds to cross the river at the places where they always have. The sheer crush of numbers pushes the first gnus into the water and into the jaws of the patient ones that lie like trout for the flies to settle. A saurian can latch onto a gnu and twist it around in the water until a piece is torn off. This is swallowed wholesale—and if it's the head, horns and all.

After having run the gauntlet with the crocodiles, the gnus must be constantly on the watch for lions, who also appreciate their flesh. Gnus are born on the move and must be able to run in about three minutes, since hyenas are always near. Female gnus will charge at hyenas and lions to protect a calf. Illness and lack of water accompany the herds and cause further decimation. Despite all this, the ubiquitous blue wildebeest remains an important species in the food chain for the survival of the predators and carrion eaters.

The blue wildebeest has a dull, bluish gray coat with some black stripes superimposed on it and a black tail. The long, sad-looking clown's face is black, and the horns are first carried out horizontally from the skull before sweeping upward. This is a wary animal to hunt, since it has many predators. Its instincts have been honed to perfection over the millennia. The wildebeest is capable of taking a big bullet and clearing off. Like other game, a wounded wildebeest is dangerous; as always, shoot straight at the heart and shoulders.

Hunting the Blue Wildebeest: One the Lions and Crocodiles Never Got

We had been hunting in Mpumalanga, South Africa. It had been hard. We had done it all right and it had come out all wrong. We had even given up hunting wildebeest—and yet we had been successful. That's hunting. Now, as the Jeep bumped, squeaked, and kidney-jolted us home, I looked the bull over, using my flashlight. It was lying in the back trailer, its tongue lolling out at me impudently. The small hole in the centre of its chest was like a red button and bore witness to a good shot under difficult circumstances. The great flap of skin hanging off his raw meat rump bore witness to a drama that I could only speculate on. I'll tell you about it.

The day was dying rapidly and soon the reddening sun would slide below the western horizon and be gone. It had been a vexing day: We had seen few animals and even less of the blue wildebeest that we were seeking. We suspected that lions had moved in and had scared everything into hiding, and we had been right. Normally, the zebras, impalas, and other animals were everywhere. You saw them just behind bushes, drinking easily at water holes or standing in the shade of trees. They stared at the Jeep with casual interest and went back to what they had been doing as it passed by. This day everything had a large dose of jitters. Then we found the lion spoor. We were not hunting cats and hoped that we would not come into a situation with them that necessitated arbitration with a bullet, since we had no license.

We were now driving along the track that the lions had walked along about half an hour before, according to Wellington, our tracker. We came to a place where the lions' pug marks in the sand showed where they had gone off in different directions. Farther on, we saw them, flicking their tails in agitation and snarling with each other. We stopped and watched. The big male was maneless, not uncommon here, and the other lions were females or immature; there were eight all told. Without warning the big male launched a vicious attack on a juvenile. We saw paws flashing and raking kicks from assorted back legs. Pieces of hide flew, and the younger lion ran off into the bushes. I turned to my PH.

"The mood they are in is likely to get either them or us into trouble."

"You bet. Let's call it a day. It's getting dark, anyway, and I doubt we will find anything now what with all the noise those damn cats are creating. They are scaring the wits out of everything in a five-mile radius. Tomorrow's another day," he answered, accelerating the Jeep away.

The bush was now acquiring that monotone, grayish colour, just before the blackout of night, that makes game spotting impossible. Above our heads we heard urgent tapping on the roof of the Jeep. Wellington, who always sat outside, leaned over and pointed into the bush as he whispered tersely through the window.

"Wildebeest."

We peered into the gloom and could just make out a dark, grayish shape, standing with head hung low, under a tree. It seemed reluctant to run. Wellington confirmed that this was our wildebeest. Don't ask me how he knew. I got out of the Jeep, chambered a bullet, and followed him. We had gotten to within about eighty metres when the wildebeest turned to face us. The only chance I had was to shoot into the chest. The crash of the rifle, the fall of the animal, and the *thuck* sound of the bullet striking all happened in the space of a second.

My PH and Wellington were still clapping me on the back when the wildebeest jumped up and was gone. The sweetness of success turned to corrosive acid in my guts; we had a wounded animal, it was night, and lions were around. We went back to the Jeep to get a light (it was necessary, by now) and set off to check the spoor. Wellington soon found blood, and his shadow danced like a demon as he followed the gleam of pink, frothy lung blood to where the wildebeest lay, not far away.

We were surprised to find that a large flap of skin hung down from its rump and that a smaller piece of hide was missing entirely from its withers. Deep red scratches were scored into its side as well. The lions had apparently only just missed pulling down this bull. Despite its escape it had been doomed, since the smell of blood would have drawn hyenas like dogs to a lamppost. If it managed to survive the night, flies would have laid their eggs on the raw, red meat by first light, and infection and maggots would have finished off what the lions had started.

Black Wildebeest (*Connochaetes gnou*)

As a species, the black wildebeest is unique to South Africa. At one time, vast herds of them existed in the Orange Free State. Then came a period of uncontrolled slaughter. The herds were so decimated that they survived only in a few isolated pockets, on private farmland. At the last moment, thanks to game management, the black wildebeest, like the North American bison, was plucked from the abyss of extinction. It was progressively reintroduced into its former habitat, wherever this was found on farmland. The animal does not exist in the wilds anymore and is encountered only on large areas of well-protected land, were it can, and must, be selectively hunted.

The black wildebeest is, as its name would imply, black. It carries a forward-curving set of horns and a long, horselike white tail, giving it its other name: the white-tailed gnu. The animal is not as large or as heavy as the blue wildebeest. A mature bull will not weigh more than two hundred kilograms. It has a stubby, vertical, brownish white mane and a large bushel of black hair sticking up on its nose. Beneath its neck is a long beard.

If the appearance of this animal is astonishing, its behaviour is comical. Black wildebeest tend to keep well together and will suddenly stop eating, appear to have a mass epileptic fit, jump in the air, toss their heads, flick their tails, and run off. Just as suddenly, they will stop their headlong gallop, buck like horses at a rodeo, shake their manes, snort in surprise, and then resume eating the grass as if nothing had happened. But then, nothing had. This behaviour has earned them the name "old fools of the veld." The animal is, however, no fool and is extremely wary and difficult to approach. Add to this bullet insensitivity and you have a challenging time ahead, if you choose to hunt it.

Hunting the Black Wildebeest: Foolish Capers in the Highveld

The black wildebeest is less cosmopolitan than the related blue wildebeest and prefers windswept and bleak rock-strewn terrain. Such a place exists in the highveld, about two hundred kilometres due east from Pretoria, South Africa, and it was there that we intended to hunt an old fool. At the end, we were nearly the fools.

The sullen gray clouds were low in the sky and the howling wind relentlessly pushed banks of them on before it. The region of Dullstroom is reputed to have the bleakest climate in the whole of South Africa. I watched the clouds rushing across the sky, pulled my warm rainproof jacket around me, and agreed. The herd of thirty or more black wildebeests, now high up on a plateau, were enjoying the wild windy weather as well as this new game they were playing with us. Let me tell you about it. We had previously approached to within two hundred metres and then one had seen us, causing pandemonium in their ranks before they all went hell-for-leather away over the boulders.

We had waited and tried approaching again. This time the wildebeests were on the lookout for us, and we got only to within three hundred metres before they kicked their collective hoofs in the air and went to another vantage point. We watched them come to a halt and then scanned the beasts over with our binoculars. The bull we sought was to the left of the herd, and he too was enjoying the game. He shook his mane and jumped up on all fours, coming down in the same spot. We tried again, this time getting to within four hundred metres (yes, they were learning fast) before they had a Derby gallop to the other end of the property. It was evident that we would have to employ other tactics.

The wind increased in intensity and quickly shepherded the woolly black-sheep clouds across the sky. It also pushed us around rudely. An hour later—it was now three in the afternoon—we set off to get within shooting distance. The wind had increased from storm to gale force, and the going was difficult since the gusts were now quite capable of blowing one over. The clouds were darker and rain threatened. We crawled over the last boulder and peeped across from our vantage point. The black wildebeests were all facing the wind to offer it the least chance of buffeting them. Skirting around to get broadside, we got into position. I estimated the distance to be 250 metres. The distance was about the maximum for me and this .375 H&H Magnum rifle-bullet combination, but there was no other way to approach our quarry. We were becoming tired of seeing their white tails streaming out behind them.

I lay down so that I could steady my rifle, but the gusts of wind still pushed it with invisible hands. The image of the bull danced about as wildly in the telescopic sight as it did in real life. I turned the magnification down to make viewing a little easier. It did. The bull was still there. I aimed a little high on the humped shoulder to compensate for the fall of the bullet; at 250 metres it would be about twenty centimetres. I squeezed off the shot, raising a shower of rock-splinter shrapnel from behind the bull's rump. The height was correct, but the lateral drift of the bullet caused by the wind—which, by now had increased to hurricane force—had carried it away. The wildebeests ran off, not appreciating my marksmanship. I felt like running off, as well, because I didn't appreciate my aim, either. We gave up for that day.

The next morning the wind abated, but the cold rain still stung our faces like nettles. Nevertheless, we fools set off searching the desolate, blasted landscape again. We found the wildebeests in their old place and were able to stalk down to about 150 metres. The bull remained where it was as the Silvertip bullet took him through the shoulders. The others took off, kicking their heels in the air, white tails flowing behind them. *They* were no fools.

Giraffe
(*Giraffa camelopardalis*)

Giraffes are fascinating big-game animals. They have such a peculiar shape that they look as if they belong on another planet. Standing on average over five metres tall, they are the tallest living mammals. Their great height makes necessary a series of special valves to regulate the flow of blood. Like most other mammals, they have seven neck vertebrae. The old bulls have short but thick parallel horns that end in blunt, bald stubs. The baldness comes from fighting. The cows have thinner, longer horns, often decorated at the top with a tuft of wispy black hair. At the end of the tail there are long, wire-tough, black hairs, similar to those of the elephant. The hide is a beautiful pattern of rich cream, white, black, and chocolate brown.

The giraffe is specialized to reach the tops of the trees, where it uses its nearly half-metre-long furry tongue like an anteater's to sweep up the tender leaves and shoots. Bulls exceed one tonne in weight, and that's plenty of bull. They fight each other by putting their necks together and pushing.

Contacting with the swing of the long necks gives a powerful slap. Such activities are called "necking," but there is nothing gentle about it. At birth, the single young can weigh up to seventy kilograms and be one-metre-seventy high. It is born about four hundred and fifty days after mating. It is ready to go after Mama twenty minutes after birth. Its horn stubs are present at birth. Ouch!

The giraffe is cloven-hoofed, and the size (large) and consistency (hard) of those appendages will convince you that they are deadly weapons. Giraffes are docile and inoffensive animals, but if they are cornered they are quite capable of neatly kicking the head off whatever has raised their ire. The great front hoofs can lash out with surprising speed and smash through flesh and bone like a steam hammer.

At one time many giraffes were killed for their meat and attractive hide. However, as the placid animals were brought onto protected game ranches they have bred and increased in number, making necessary some hunting to maintain healthy populations and good age structures. I do believe that giraffes are incapable of swimming. Perhaps they are top heavy, but with that periscope neck they could have a go at playing submarines.

Hunting the Giraffe: A Tall Ticking Off

We were in the Hoedspruit area in Mpumalanga, Republic of South Africa, and, as it was April, the bush was still thick and visibility was down to ten metres at places. Not good if you want to hunt small game, but then, we were hunting big game, or at least, the tallest game in the world.

The landowner had about twenty-four giraffes on his property, but the age and population structure of them was far from ideal. Too many bulls were chasing the cows and a lot of necking was going on, if you get what I mean. There was one old boy who was gray in the muzzle and surely short in the tooth, the result of about two decades of chewing acacia and other assorted greenery. Despite its age the giraffe still kept up with three other bulls, and we now stood watching them all striding away for the third time that day. Despite our care in stalking and watching out for the wind, the giraffes, with their penetrating binocular eye power, had seen us. Giraffes have the most acute vision and widest field of view of any land mammal. Despite this, we doggedly took up the spoor.

We crept up toward the place where the bush had been cleared for a small landing strip. Across the clearing, about one hundred metres away, the giraffes stood feeding off the top leaves of a patch of acacia trees. The bull we wanted was behind the group of three bulls and so was shielded from any bullet that might be sent its way. We had taken great care to reach the position that we were now in, and the hawk-eyed giraffes hadn't yet suspected our presence. We lay watching them pull the leaves into their mouths. Time moved on and the giraffes moved on with it, slowly browsing along, searching for greenery. I felt a tick bore into my leg but couldn't move for fear of betraying our presence. The sensation was like that of a small but red-hot pinprick. We followed the giraffes using the leopard-crawling technique that makes your knees raw and turns your hands and elbows into bloody steaks. It was worth it, though, because they still hadn't seen us. Our luck was holding, praise Mr. Murphy. We got nearer. They saw us. Curse Mr. Murphy.

There was now no time to play "Catch me if you can." We had had enough of it for that day, so I stood up and threw the rifle to my shoulder. The bull was broadside about one hundred metres away from me, moving along from my right to left. I got the cross hairs of the scope on its shoulder, swung with the moving beast and then, judging the speed and time of flight, led out a bit in front of its chest and squeezed the trigger. The *dupf* sound of the .375 H&H Magnum Silvertip bullet strike came back, over the sharp crash of the rifle fire, and immediately all the giraffes shifted into high gear; all, that is, except one. The stricken bull peeled off to its right and moved down into low gear. I chambered another bullet and followed up. The giraffe was now swaying like an inebriate, and its neck was horizontal as death came. It sat down, legs tucked beneath it and neck level with the ground. I had come to within thirty metres of it. Keeping clear to avoid a bit of necking, I placed a second bullet in its chest. The giraffe's great motor switched off.

It's amazing how big giraffes are. In the zoo or at a distance you get the impression of a delicate animal, but right up close you get another. The great camel-like head of this specimen, topped off with bald horns, was covered with ticks. The pea-sized pests, gorged with blood, festooned the eyelids like metallic beads inserted there for ornament, as is done in African body piercing.

It took some time to rough-cape the giraffe and cut up the meat. Natives who were working on the concession appeared like magic to help with the butchery. After cutting up the meat and distributing presents of the gory stuff to the helpers, we took a drink of beer from ring-pull cans. It was warm, flat, and tasted tinny. We drank it anyway.

At base we finished off the caping, learning that giraffe skin is tough. Four or five strokes with a razor-sharp skinning knife were enough to transform it to a blunt butter spreader. The neck skin was like cured leather. After a long time and more beer (still metallic-tasting but cooler), the cape and backskin were spread out and covered with salt. I paid the native skinners a generous tip, and we went to have a bite to eat and to crawl into bed.

The next day I awoke to an itching sensation on my leg. The tick that had hitched a ride on me the day before was now a very fat passenger, bloated with blood. I managed to remove it, proboscis and all. The place where the blasted thing had banqueted itched like merry hell for the rest of the hunt. And for weeks afterward, too.

Gray or Common Duiker (*Sylvicapra grimmia*)

This common, adaptable, and hardy browsing antelope reaches a metre in length, is about seventy centimetres at the shoulder, and might attain twenty kilograms in weight. Interestingly enough, the duiker will eat meat in the form of insects, frogs, and carrion. As its name implies, it is a nondescript grayish colour; the underside lightens to a yellowish beige. The males have short, sharp, straight black horns up to about twelve centimetres long. Females, who are larger than the males, may occasionally carry small vestiges of horns. Usually a single young is born after two hundred days of gestation. The males have big patches on the side of their face that are scent glands. Gray duikers might not be big or flamboyant representatives of the African fauna, but they are difficult to hunt because of their small size. They are quick and have fast reactions and plenty of stamina (they can run for ages over rough terrain). Add to this their ability to vanish at any time, and you should get the idea how difficult it is to hunt them.

Not Hunting the Gray Duiker: One Round to Me, at Last, Mr. Murphy!

I have often found that when you are hunting a specific species, you don't find it. This has happened to me so often that I believe it to be a real phenomenon, similar to the well-known Murphy's Law. Look for impala and you'll see kudu staring at you from every bush with the nonchalance born of knowing that they are not on the list today. The impalas will be nowhere. Hunt kudu and the reverse is true. Look for warthog and bushbuck will jump into the back of the Jeep with you to help with the spotting. Once, as I was crawling along the ground in the last stage of a rhino stalk, a warthog came right up and stared at me. It then gave a grunt of disapproval and trotted off in that stuffy, self-important manner warthogs have. I noticed this "seek and ye shall *not* find" effect so often that I went to the extent of stating that I was hunting, say warthog, whilst it was impala that I was after. That didn't work, either, since the result was that I then usually saw nothing. Murphy had struck again. Such are the vagaries of hunting.

Once, in Hoedspruit, Republic of South Africa, I was hunting for a trophy warthog, one with tusks that would curl out wide and then come in over the top of the snout and nearly touch there in an ivory circle. Tusks to make even an elephant jealous. We had given up and were driving home, as it was getting late for warthog to be out. Suddenly my PH stopped the Jeep and pointed to a gray patch under a wait-a-bit thornbush, about eighty metres away.

"I say, I think you should jump out and insert a piece of lead into that old gray duiker; it's carrying horns a bit too long for its well-being," he whispered intently.

I was immediately out of the Jeep. The rifle said, "Bang," and the little duiker died and said nothing. We walked up to the animal and studied its horns; definitely big, but how big? The tape measure was applied and the points ascribed. It exceeded the minimum requirement for a place in the "Book" by plenty. That made it indeed an exceptional, trophy gray duiker. It was my first. Hell, I wasn't even hunting duiker, and I got a high-scoring one. I shudder to think what would have happened if I had been really looking for a trophy gray duiker. Have a drink on me, Mr. Murphy!

Bushpig
(*Potamochoerus porcus*)

Bushpig are rarely seen, because of their nocturnal habits. They are widely distributed in southern Africa, especially in agricultural areas. The elusive, bristled beast with long tufts of hair on its ears is a common animal that causes much destruction to crops. The bushpig can reach about one and a half metres in length and nearly a metre at the shoulder, weighing one hundred and twenty kilograms or more. Its tusks, used for grubbing food and defense, reach in total eight centimetres for the upper and about sixteen centimetres for the lower ones. It possesses good senses and can run and swim well. The sow gives birth to about four piglets four months after mating. Bushpigs are very dangerous animals when wounded or cornered.

Hunting the Bushpig: Be Prepared

Farmers whose crops have been "attended to" by bushpigs tend to get high blood pressure and can be prone to break out in livid welts. Such is the devastation that these beasts can inflict. The farmers, as well as taking medicine to lower their blood pressure, have also developed various ingenious ways to reduce bushpig numbers, but the crafty critters always learn to avoid poison or traps. A method that still remains popular with the farmers, as well as the pigs, is the use of beer-soaked maize corn. The pigs readily take the intoxicating "gravy" on the maize meal and become tipsy, often falling asleep at the dinner table, so to speak. The inebriates are caught and dispatched accordingly. Put it down to the perils of drinking.

Another way to trick the pigs is to hide in a tree and imitate the distress call of a piglet. If a herd is nearby they may come to investigate, thus affording a quick shooter a chance to shoot. Bushpigs may also be shot on a leopard bait, placed on the ground, since they are partial to a bit of meat. Still another way to hunt them is to chase them with dogs. Whichever way you go about it, hunting the bushpig is a tough proposition for anything on four or two legs. The balance on bushpig hunts, with dogs driving them out of thick bush, is usually two or three dead or badly tusked dogs for each pig seen or shot: a humbling lesson in porcine pugnacity if ever there was one. There are bushpig specialists who have dogs just for hunting these terrible tuskers, but many canines end up slit open like a popped sausage in a frying pan. You see, courage is simply not enough to protect a dog's flanks from tusks like cut-throat razors.

Whether one gets a bushpig depends a lot on luck. OK, all hunting depends on luck, but with bushpig you particularly need that extra pinch of luck. You also need to defy the laws of averages and probability combined, and you need persistence and hope. I can tell you now that, except for persistence and hope, I have had neither of the above-mentioned ingredients in the case of bushpig, although I've seen them and nearly was able to shoot, once. It was not to be. Read on if you want a lesson on how not to do it, and to learn the meaning of "It's not over until it's finished."

Our position was north of Johannesburg on the Vaalwater concession, the Republic of South Africa. The area of bush contained plenty of plains game of many varieties, but my PH and I were trying to get a leopard and had been failing. On this particular night we had remained in the blind longer than usual since a big silver dollar moon beamed down onto the place where our warthog bait was. The moonlight would have been sufficient to allow a shot. We had waited, staring at the gray shape of the bait, but only a small civet cat came to supper. About ten o'clock we tired of the cold and the waiting and decided to leave. We packed our things up and started down the wide trail to where the Jeep was parked, some three kilometres away. Our black helper went first, carrying the blankets (we couldn't leave them in the blind because baboons had already raided us once, purloining a bag of boiled sweets and a roll of toilet paper (what the hell did they want that for?). My PH came behind us, playing his torchlight in front to spot snakes, should there be any lying on the path.

We got back, and I put my unloaded rifle in its bag. First mistake. Andrees, our black helper, jumped onto the back of the Jeep. I went inside. Second mistake. My PH set the Jeep in motion and off we bounced down the long track out of the property. We were talking about the desolate leopard situation when the headlights picked up a herd of grayish brown creatures, walking down the track.

"Bushpigs!" exclaimed my PH, applying the brakes so sharply that my face came very near to the windscreen. "Get out, and settle one's hash."

I snatched the door open and piled out. The clever bushpigs had started to run. Andrees had already unzipped my rifle and now thrust it into my hands. I brought the rifle up, but the magnification on the telescopic sight was too high. The pigs had left the light cone of the headlights in the meantime. My PH drove the sixty metres or so to the corner whilst I chased and stumbled after the Jeep. There I was, running on a dark dirt track, visibility at zero; there was no time to think about snakes now.

Coming to a stop, I saw some pigs looking back toward us. They were uncertain as to where the light was coming from. I put the cross hairs on one and squeezed the trigger. The sharp click of the firing pin striking an empty chamber was loud. Of course, I had unloaded and had, in the heat of the moment, forgotten to reload. The bushpigs stayed a second more and then trotted off. Disgusted with myself, I handed my rifle back to Andrees and climbed back into the Jeep.

"Well?" asked my PH, with raised eyebrows.

"I was inside the Jeep and the rifle was packed away and unloaded. The scope's magnification was too high, and the pigs cleared off," I replied, pretending not to care.

"Now, let that be a lesson to you. Never pack your rifle away until we are out of the concession, and it's better to be ready for anything at any time in this game. Like boy scouts, the client should be prepared for anything. What's more, it's never over until it's finished."

I cast him a withering look and climbed out of the Jeep, his hooting laughter following me. I joined Andrees up on the top of the Jeep, unpacked my rifle, and shoved a cartridge into the chamber, putting the safety on. I was ready for 'em now. The trouble was that I never saw another bushpig that time around. You win another round, Mr. Murphy! (To put the record straight, we had a special permit to shoot at night with artificial light. The bushpigs were classified as vermin because of the destruction of the crops.)

Bushpig: If at First You Don't Succeed, Try, Try, and Try Again

I continued to want a bushpig, and, despite previous near and disappointing encounters, I was not prepared to give up. Hunting is, among other things, also about going for it and never giving up.

The place was Nylstroom in the North Province of South Africa, about a three-hour car drive north of Johannesburg. The time was early July, and it was winter. My PH for this hunt had assured me that there were bushpigs on the concession and that they were less nocturnal than is usually expected. We now stood looking at the scraps of blue wildebeest before us. Sometime during the previous night the cow had lain down and died the death of the very old. Soon after, jackals and hyenas had come to pay their last respects. Our black tracker, Johannis, was now pointing to another interesting spoor in the sand. Bushpigs had also visited here and had obviously taken part in the feast. This gave us hope, but a few tracks in the sand are still a long way from trophy bushpig in the salt. My PH turned to me.

"The bushpigs around here seem to enjoy their share of meat. You see, we have many meat hunters in here, and we take off at least two hundred blesbok per season for meat and biltong processing. The insides are left in the bush for the carnivores, who are then less inclined to attack livestock. The bushpigs have also learned that it's easier to find the meat and offal than to chase it. I propose that we go and get some more meat and bring it here later tonight. We can stalk in tomorrow morning by first light, and we might just be lucky enough to catch a bushpig still feeding."

"All right," I responded. "Let's go and process something old into meat so that we can get a new trophy!"

Later that day we placed the carcass of an impala ram next to the now stinking remains of the wildebeest. We left to have an early supper and night. Tomorrow we would be up well before dawn.

We set off by foot the next morning. The chill of the predawn was sufficient to cause light frosting on the ground. Johannis led the way as surely as if the path had been illuminated. I had, as usual, my .375 H&H Magnum, loaded with Silvertip bullets. We had a walk of about seven kilometres before us and were grateful for the movement to help shake off the biting cold. The darkness gave way, at first coyly, to the insistence of the day, and when we got to within two kilometres of the place it was already shooting light. Taking great care to make no noise, mouse-footing it slowly and checking the wind, we made our final approach.

Johannis was the first to spot them. There were three bushpigs some three hundred metres from us. They were grubbing around the carcasses, most probably mopping up meat and maggots. What a breakfast. We closed in and the last two hundred metres took time, but the bushpigs still hadn't winded us. I got up to a stunted thornbush and placed my rifle in the fork of a branch. The telescopic sight was turned up to 10X, and I saw clearly the big, flat warts on the face of the boar. I took in the fact that the bushpig has a thick coat of light brown bristles and a magnificent silver ridge of bristles going down its back. More attractive than the warthog, in any case.

The boar was standing broadside enough, and I squeezed off the bullet, which impacted its shoulder region a fraction of a second later. The boar dropped where it was, and the two sows, back bristles erect, came over to see what their old man was doing, twitching about on the ground like that. We remained where we were and the sows milled around, undecided what to do. Johannis whistled. They cocked their heads and then, tails vertical, ran off into the thick cover. We went over to the old boar. It was a big one, all right: 90 kilograms of prime pork, and the tusks poking out of his snout got him a permanent mention in Rowland Ward's book.

Klipspringer
(*Oreotragus oreotragus*)

The klipspringer (literally, cliff jumper) is found as a single species in rocky terrain and mountains from Nigeria to Angola, the Central African Republic, Ethiopia, Namibia, and South Africa. It is a small animal, just over a metre long and half a metre high at the shoulder. It is a browser, but where it lives there is usually not much on which to browse. Only the males have horns; they are stubby and straight, rarely exceeding fourteen centimetres in length. The animal jumps with great sureness and speed from one boulder to another on the tips of its hoofs.

The klipspringer is in many ways similar to the chamois *(Rupicapra rupicapra)* of the Alpine regions of Europe, in as much as it can also whistle up a sharp warning to members of its group when danger appears. Its coat is most unusual with respect to both colour and texture. The pelage is tinged yellow and olive green and speckled with brown; the belly is white. The coat hairs are stubby and bristlelike and can be bent like elastic glass fibres. The thickness of its coat protects the animal from the cold of the mountain air and also serves to cushion the frequent jarring contacts the animal makes with its rocky environment.

Hunting the Klipspringer: Long Climb for a Short-Horned Ballet Star

We were still on the Nylstroom concession, three hours' drive north of Johannesburg, South Africa. After having experienced success, at last, with bushpig hunting, I got overconfident and one evening, suitably lubricated with good red Cape wine, expressed the wish to hunt a klipspringer. After all, I'd heard so much about these interesting animals, and I knew that hunting them was difficult. The meat of the klipspringer, I'd also heard, was very good, and I was getting tired of warthog.

The next day we drove to the base of a brooding mountain of the Waterberg range. I looked up at the steeply forbidding terrain, strewn with rocks, and began to have second thoughts about the desirability of having a klipspringer in my trophy room. The great sky of Africa was the purest blue of a sapphire; the sun was already a pool of boiling mercury in it—and it was only 8:30 A.M. My PH and the tracker, Johannis, hoisted their backpacks filled with sandwiches and liquid refreshments. Both my PH and I shouldered our rifles and we set off, following a small game trail ever upward. Within an hour we were all well basted with sweat, and the constant lifting of legs and energy-robbing circumventing of boulders was evident in the form of muscle cramp. Still we went upward, seeking the way to the summit. We had been climbing for three hours now and stopped for a much-needed refreshment pause. We sank wearily to the ground and rummaged open the backpacks. Never before had a bottle of crystal-clear water looked so good. The taste was even better as the liquid slid down our parched throats. It would have been easy to simply watch the sun slide back down the sky and to give up. But hunting is about never giving up. Hunting is about going that further mile.

We were nearly at the top and stopped, momentarily, to take our bearings. Suddenly Johannis jumped back and pointed out a snake that had been sunning itself on a rock, digesting at the same time the lizard whose back legs and tail still stuck out of its mouth. The snake was of a greenish brown colour and had a yellow stripe running down its side. We didn't take time to identify it. We swigged down some more water and went on.

The watcher on the rock pinnacle was an old female klipspringer. She blew the whistle on us and all the trains, about ten of them, left the station with flashes of furry alacrity. We cursed Mr. Murphy roundly while waiting before taking up the grueling climb to higher regions.

I now leopard-crawled in, rifle in front of me. I was trying to reach a stunted bush where I could obtain cover and support for my rifle. The old male klipspringer stood on a small boulder on the other side of the valley, about one hundred and twenty metres away. He was opposite me and broadside and poised daintily on his ballet-shoe hoofs so that it was difficult to estimate the horn length. It was certainly an old klipspringer, but the horns did not appear to be exceptional.

The telescopic rifle sights were now fixed on the point of its shoulder as I adjusted my position by the bush. I took a deep breath, and, when it was half expired, fired. I actually saw the shower of greenish hair fan out from behind the klipspringer as the Silvertip bullet in calibre .375 H&H Magnum exited its far shoulder. It was instantly dead. Strangely enough, there were no other klipspringers around; we were expecting a few to slip into their ballet shoes and dance it all the way to the mountaintop. We waited awhile and then went down the side of the valley and climbed up the opposite side.

The area where the klipspringer lay was spattered with blood and strewn with thousands of hairs. The bristlelike nature of them must be felt to be appreciated. The necessary photographs and congratulations were performed, and the tape measure verified that the klipspringer was just within the limit for entry into Rowland Ward's book.

The klipspringer was gutted and placed carefully into a backpack so as not to cause more hair loss. The way down the mountain was even more arduous than the way up, and the constant pressure on the nails of our big toes was excruciating. I'll bet you a stiff drink that any klipspringers observing our descent must have laughed to see our hobbling and unsure steps on their stony stage.

Spotted Hyena
(*Crocuta crocuta*)

Hyenas are just as well known as elephants, leopards, Cape buffaloes, lions, and zebras. Why? It is not the size of *mpisi*, for it is not bigger than a large dog. It is not the prettiness of its fur, for it has a nondescript dirty-yellow fur with a scattering of black spots. It is not the shape, for it has hindquarters that appear too low on the ground, giving it a crippled appearance and gait. It is not the trophy; it hasn't got one. It is not the visible differences between the males or females, as there are none: Both even have penislike appendages dangling between their back legs. (Robert Ruark, in his book *Use Enough Gun*, ridiculed the hyena as being a cowardly thing and a hermaphrodite, capable of changing its sex, and went on to destroy much of the remaining character the hyena may have had. Much of what he wrote about the hyena was wrong, but it reflected the general state of knowledge and the attitude of people toward hyenas in the 1950s.) It is not the speed of the hyena, for it cannot do more than fifty kilometres per hour over a short distance. It might, however, be known for its endurance, for it can run many kilometres at a medium pace. It might also be known for the most powerful jaws in the animal kingdom, which can crush an elephant's thigh bone as though it were a stick of celery. It might be known for its excellent night vision. But I believe it is known for none of these things.

It is the sounds that *mpisi* makes that has got it a special place in the fauna of Africa. The sounds, which range from a gentle *whoo hoop* to boisterous chortles and hysterical giggling, much like a crowd of school kids on a day trip, are always to be heard out in the bush—always, when something dies. Or is killed. It is difficult for people to separate the laughing sound of the hyena from the basic human sounds of joy or mirth. The hyena does not know these sentiments. The sounds are just coincidental. For a long time the spotted hyena was reviled as a stinking, filthy eater of carrion and an opportunist that occasionally pulled newly born animals from their mothers. True, the hyena commits these acts, but it is just as Mother Nature intended. The continent of Africa has an efficient sanitation corps, since our spotted friend with the varied diet sees that nothing, animal or human, goes to waste.

There is another side to the life of the hyena. It has a strictly matriarchal society (the offspring of the dominant female have the best chance to survive). The family clan cooperates as an active and deadly hunting pack, and, above all, they are the sworn enemies of the lion. Only recently has it been documented just how efficient hyenas are in hunting (as opposed to scavenging). Even more impressive is the bitter, total, bloody, and constant war they wage against lions (and, take it from me, the lions reciprocate). The dirty knaves of the bush can make life very difficult for the king of beasts.

There are two species of hyena, the spotted and the brown. The latter (*Hyaena brunnea*) is solitary and has a lionlike mane and is rarely seen. Despite looking in many respects like a dog, the hyena is a unique species probably more closely related to the cat family. The males are smaller than the females and are submissive to them. When hunting, a great deal of teamwork and cooperation is evident.

Hyenas have no enemies except for man, lions, and, occasionally, themselves. A clan of hyenas will kill and eat a hyena from another family without compunction. The young will commit fratricide to improve their social status, and the matriarch hyena will kill young hyenas that are not her own. Family life must be a very nerve-jangling affair for hyenas! In many places in South Africa, the lions have been shot out in favour of the cattle farmer and the game rancher. The cats cannot be tolerated because of their predations. Of course, in earlier times there was much more land available and fewer cattle, but all that has changed. With the lions mostly gone now from farm areas, the hyenas have one enemy less. Thus, they must be kept down to tolerable levels using the rifle. It is worth mentioning here that the hyena plays an important role in the religious beliefs of many African tribes, and the indigenous peoples have a great respect for *mpisi*. This respect may also be connected with fear of the creatures, which they know are quite capable of killing and devouring anything in the bush, including human beings. Some tribes use the hyena's services as an undertaker. The dead are left in the bush and *mpisi* comes and eats them up. Nice and clean.

Hunting the Spotted Hyena: The Last Laugh

We were in the Gravelotte region of the North Province of South Africa and May had just begun. The days were warm but the nights already had the chill of winter in them. The game was scarce and scared because the clan of *mpisi* had moved in. The area had had trouble with lions in surrounding farmland, and the *mpisi* had followed the lions, for they profit from their kills. The lions had been shot out but the *mpisi* remained. Now it was time to shoot some of them out, as well.

Our plan was to hunt the hyenas during the day. This demanded some special tactics, since our friends with the big teeth and viselike jaws are basically nocturnal. However, if one can put a large enough piece of meat down for them, they will not be able to finish it before morning. The hyenas will then remain near the carcass to keep other scavengers off. A careful approach is then needed to shoot a hyena. The ethics of hunting and respect for the constellation of the hyena clan demand that the leading matriarch not be shot. The sole purpose of this hunt was to reduce their numbers but to leave the matriarch the chance to lead the rest of the clan away to a safer area. We hoped that they would oblige us, because we had just shot an old, broken-down cow waterbuck for their going-away supper.

The moon was a thin sliver of silver set in a black sky, the stars winked down on the bush, and now the creatures moved in on the bait. Using caution born from experience, they had first circled, testing every nuance of the situation. The *mpisi* had appeared like silent ghosts. The gentle sough of the wind in the trees was even louder than they were. The matriarch decided that all was clear and, breaking the silence with a chattering sound of mirth, went to the carcass. The bait, which had been put down by us the previous day, had begun to stink, and the hyenas had come, as always, to perform their necromantic duties on it. When something is ill, dying, or dead, the hyenas will know of it and come. The rest of the clan joined the female, and the waterbuck started to vanish under the snapping action of the steel-sprung jaws.

The coming of day had caused a smudge of orange to be raised in the morning sky as we set off to examine the waterbuck bait. Our trackers, Thomas and Joseph, sat in the back of the Jeep as we bounced our way deep into the bushland to see if the *mpisi* had been to supper. A dusting of icing-sugar frost had formed on the wild aloes during the night and even the birds were quiet, for it was still early. We stopped about two kilometres away from the place, stretched our legs, checked the rifles, and, skirting around, started our approach downwind. We were well positioned, as was evidenced by the stench of carrion coming from the bait to our nostrils. This is not recommended just before or after breakfast. Over the last half-kilometre or so we slowed our pace and moved in, aided by the now ever-strengthening daylight.

The high priests of necromancy were still there, lying around the remains of the totally demolished waterbuck. They had taken their communion feast to the limit, as evidenced by their bloated bellies. I could pick out various individuals, and the largest one, the matriarch, was easily identifiable. Picking out another hyena, I put the cross hairs of the scope on its shoulder, and the rifle went off.

The clan went off also, into cover, laughing insanely and casting distrustful looks over their sloping-down backs. We found no blood. Not a single ruby bead of it. I had missed. I, who had shot impala from over two hundred metres, had jerked my shot and sent the bullet whistling over the back of *mpisi*. I had read that folks go mad when aiming at a leopard and shoot anything but the leopard. Boughs of trees are neatly amputated by bullets whilst the leopard stares in amazement at the damage and then the blind, in that order, before springing away, never to return. Hunters well versed in the art of shooting straight have missed elephants from a few metres' distance. How is all this possible? The answer is beyond me. Put it down to NPS, or near proximity syndrome (at least that sounds scientific). If it's not NPS then it has something to do with old man Murphy and his law, again.

In case you are wondering, no, I never got a hyena, and maybe everybody else misses 'em too. This could be the very reason why they laugh.

Warthog (*Phacochoerus aethiopicus*)

Warthogs are common animals in South Africa and Namibia. They are decidedly ugly beasts, with their sparsely bristled bodies and warty faces. They are dangerous, as well, with their terrible tusks. The boars have four big warts on their faces and the sows two smaller ones. They are not large as game animals go, usually about twenty to thirty kilograms in weight and about sixty centimetres at the shoulder, fully grown.

The warthog is a diurnal animal, found only during the day grubbing for food or wallowing in mud (nothing quite like it for cooling the blood). Unfortunately for warthogs, lions and leopards like a bit of pork now and then. Unfortunately for the lions and leopards, warthogs can be a tough nut to crack (or pig to bite), since they have a set of tusks like ivory sabres and the courage to match. Warthogs are feisty animals that will not hesitate to slit anything (hunters included) wide open if cornered. Dogs are usually sent packing in various states of severe injury. At night, warthogs reverse into their earth burrows to make sure that any uninvited nocturnal predator will first meet with tusks honed to razor sharpness rather than a tender leg of pork.

Hunting the Warthog: What Clicking Scalpels Can Do

The gray-black clouds were piled upon each other in smothering layers and the cold wind whistled through the branches now sparsely dressed in the drab dry leaves of winter. It was August in Mpumalanga, South Africa, and not a good day to hunt. We were out looking for something to fill the meat store, and an impala or warthog would have fitted the bill. My PH was driving, I was in the back of the Jeep, and, for company, I had Andrees, our black tracker and game spotter.

We had now stopped and were waiting for the magic moment when the dawn really broke the hold of night. Andrees' cigarette glowed dull red and, somewhere out in the bush, a couple of zebra stallions started up their daily belligerence. You could hear muffled thuds as hoofs thumped into flanks and the donkeylike *wyawop, wyawop, wyawop, wyawop!* braying as they agreed to disagree over the day's point of contention. We also heard something clashing horns with something else. It was not a day to hunt; everything was in a bad mood. With us in the Jeep was the Jack Russell terrier called Brakenjaan, or just "Brakkie." This little live wire of a dog would delight in chasing anything, including Cape buffalo and hyenas, on sight. The power of bluff has to be seen to be believed, and Brakkie had made it so far by the applied psychology of bluff, terror, and agility. It was amazing to see a buffalo take off, skittishly kicking its hoofs backward in the hope of connecting with the tiny black and white pugnacious pooch hard on its heels. Of course, Brakkie knew exactly the distance that he could keep and had honed his nipping skills to a fine art. He was soon to take a severe lesson in keeping a greater distance.

Andrees flicked his cigarette butt overboard in a practiced movement. It fell onto the sand in a shower of sparks and continued to glow. He then hawked up a lump of phlegm and spat it explosively overboard. It arched in the same direction as the previously jettisoned cigarette, and I guessed that he was trying to put it out. If he was, he failed. Rummaging in his overcoat pocket, he pulled out a flat and battered tin, pried the lid off with his cracked thumbnail, and took out a pinch of snuff. The powder was applied to each nostril and inhaled in one rough sniff. The Jeep sneezed and sputtered into a start and we moved off.

A boar warthog burst from out of the cover and trotted off, tail erect, to the left. The Jeep slowed and, not waiting for it to stop, I jumped out to try and get off a shot. Brakkie noted this and, no doubt fancying a bit of a run and some pork for supper, decided to help bring the quarry to bay. He sprang out of the Jeep and set off at full speed after the warthog. Warthogs do not take kindly to being disturbed and then chased by dogs. Or anything else, for that matter. Their first reaction is to try to outrun the enemy or, if a suitable burrow is available, to seek refuge. The warthog did just that. It came across an aardvark's hole and went down inside. The aardvark (*Orycteropus afer*) is a large, tubular-toothed, burrowing animal with sharp claws. Its Afrikaans name means "earth pig." Brakkie also vanished down the burrow with the warthog, and he wasn't visiting for tea, either. As I ran up, out of breath, I could hear the muffled growling of the dog and the squeals of the pig as Brakkie got stuck into it. Well, it sure did sound as if pig-sticking was going on down there. I made sure that I was ready to shoot and stood back.

The warthog had entered the aardvark's burrow head-first, because of the urgency of the situation. Brakkie had managed to get hold of its tail before it could turn around, and now a tug-of-war was going on. Judging by the squeals of indignation, I gathered that the warthog did not agree with its being forcibly separated from its tail, or any other appendage, if it came to that.

Another sound now came to me, the sharp, cut-off yelp of the dog. The next moment, a bloody-tailed warthog shot out of the burrow. It came running past me, tusks clicking like castanets. Fearing for my appendages, I ran quickly to the side. Then the hog was gone into the bush. There was no time to shoot. Brakkie was nowhere to be seen. I was now joined by my PH, and we went over to the burrow. We could hear whimpering and feared the worst. It was. Brakkie crawled up and out of the burrow slowly, for he was terribly injured.

The tusk slash had been applied with the precision of a brain surgeon's laser-guided scalpel, and the intestines were now hanging out of the dog's belly in bluish gray ropes. One look was enough to see that the dog was finished. My

PH raised his rifle, to end the dog's suffering. I looked at the dog, lying there panting, and noted that there was not much blood, except around his muzzle, since he'd nearly chewed off the warthog's tail. I could see out of the corner of my eye that my PH's rifle was on his shoulder, and soon the crash of cordite would end brave Brakkie's life. I looked at the dog again and noticed a movement; Brakkie was wagging his stumpy tail! Now a dog that can wag its tail after losing a fight with a warthog and dragging itself out of the burrow with its guts hanging out can't be all that near to cashing in its ticket. I shouted not to shoot.

"Let's get him cleaned up and see if we can't save the little devil. If we can get him over the shock stage, and if the guts are not ruptured, we stand a chance."

We got a tarpaulin from the Jeep and laid the stricken dog on it. Andrees held Brakkie's head and front paws. A quick check revealed that no intestine was ruptured; only the retaining membrane had been opened, allowing the viscera to fall out. A classic case of rupture. We washed our hands and carefully pushed the slippery, pulsing worms of guts back to where we thought they should go. Occasionally Brakkie would whimper. It must have been painful for him to have his guts rearranged for the second time that day. Taking great care to keep sand and other dirt out of the region, we managed to get everything back and stitched him up. We knew that the risk of a twisted gut, leading to agonizing peritonitis and inevitable death, was high, but we reckoned that anything was worth trying to save him. We did. After a heavy course of antibiotics and a recuperation of only a week, the dog was up and about, looking for trouble again.

Brakkie hated warthogs after this incident (which I can understand) and chased them as before; the only difference was that now he never followed them into their burrows. He developed a special tactic for when they went to ground. He would stand at the opening, bark as loudly as he could, and then lift his back leg and squirt a few jets of urine right down the entrance. A few short scratches followed with his back legs, to mark the occasion of his visit, and he would walk away, growling and stiff-legged, leaving the warthog to the pungent smell of his urine.

About a year after this incident, Brakkie was out in the bush with a small black boy. Brakkie had chased some hyenas. They turned on him, but he was outnumbered. They circled him and bit chunks of meat out of his body, eating him alive. He went down fighting, while the boy ran home to get help. There wasn't much left of the brave dog when help arrived.

Southern Mountain Reedbuck (*Redunca arundinum*)

There are three known species of reedbuck. The southern mountain reedbuck is smaller than the other species and lives in mountainous terrain. It can climb as well as a goat. It can reach thirty kilograms in weight, is about one and a half metres long, and stands a metre high at the shoulder. It has a gray coat that becomes white on the underside. The bushy tail, relatively long at forty centimetres, is white underneath and is held up as a warning signal when the animal flees. This behaviour is found generally in antelope and deer species. Only the males carry horns. Normally a single young is born, eight months after mating.

Hunting the Southern Mountain Reedbuck: An Unexpected Trophy

We had seen a small group of southern mountain reedbuck all week but had only just received permission to hunt for a ram. Now that we had permission we saw neither hide nor hair of them. That old rogue Mr. Murphy was with us again. It's always like that. The same thing has happened to me when I was hunting red hartebeest. No license, you see plenty; get a license and they're gone. Never mind, back to leopard hunting.

The last days of the hunt were coming up. We were still trying for a leopard in the North Province area of Vaalwater, South Africa. We had baited the cat with baboons, impalas, and even old donkeys, but it didn't accept our invitation to dinner. We suspected that the tomcat was love struck and busy with a lady friend, for we had seen two pairs of tracks, one small and the other large, around the bait. Obviously, the taste of love was more delicious than the mere ambrosia of assorted meats, in various states of decomposition, that we were offering.

It was the last night of my hunt, and, as usual, we walked down the long, narrow path at the bottom of the valley that led to our bait tree. We never spoke about it, but we knew that the chance of getting a leopard was now virtually zero. The mood was depressed because departure was on the morrow. We were trying to the last, however, because you never know when Mr. Murphy will decide to pack up his bags and leave you to join another unfortunate hunting party. The sun had gone below the mountains, and it was getting dark in the valley. Shadows melted with each other and crept across the land like a silent, all-engulfing oil slick, blackening all before them. We still had another kilometre or so to walk when our tracker stopped and pointed up the flank of the mountain slope.

The herd of mountain reedbuck stood watching us on poised, dainty legs from a boulder-strewn field about eighty metres away. They were sculptures in rock, not moving. I could make out the horns on one buck and, caring not for the delicate eardrums of leopards, I shot him. The crash of the rifle rolled around the valley like a thunderclap and was instantly replaced by the usual cacophony of baboon cries of protest. The buck with the hole through his neck fell down toward us, whilst the other reedbucks bounded up and away.

Our tracker went to where the buck lay and dragged him the rest of the way. It was a beautiful animal with doelike eyes, but the jet black, ringed horns, which curve forward, gave it a puckish appearance. Its gray top fur was silky and soft to the touch, and its belly was pure white, as was the lower surface of the long, rabbitlike, fluffy tail.

"Good shooting," said my PH as he searched his pockets for a tape measure and wire. "I'd just like to see how long those horns are. I've never seen any like this."

He went to work, carefully fixing one end of the measuring wire to the base of a horn and tracing it to the very tip. He then held the wire to the tape. He repeated the action with the other horn, stood up, and let out a long whistle.

"Unless Mr. Rowland Ward has increased the minimum requirements for his record book, let me be the first to congratulate you on a great trophy!"

We set about caping, and within half an hour we had the skin. It was, by now, quite dark. We sent our tracker back to the Jeep with the skin and meat. He was given instructions on how to cover the skin with salt (mountain reedbuck hide must be put in salt quickly, to avoid hairslip) and told to remain where he was until he heard a shot or we returned. We carried on to our leopard blind.

The leopard never did come that night, but who cared? I didn't because I had an unexpected trophy buck. The leopard didn't care either. He'd had other business to take care of, because we heard that some six months later a female leopard was seen playing with two cubs near to where our bait tree had been.

Springbok
(*Antidorcas marsupialis*)

The springbok is found nearly everywhere in South Africa, Namibia, Botswana, and Angola. It likes open, dry savannas. It is a relatively small antelope about one and a half metres long, standing eighty centimetres at the shoulder. It weighs up to fifty kilograms. Springboks like to jump high into the air on stiff legs, head bent down, and they appear to bounce effortlessly, like a child's rubber ball. This behaviour is called "pronking." Don't ask me why. Springboks have been clocked up to eighty kilometres per hour over a short distance, so if you want to catch one, don't try! The sandy brown coat above is separated from the white underside by a deeper, reddish brown horizontal band. Both male and female have black-ringed horns. The males usually have thicker, shorter horns. The kid is born some six months after mating. Commercial farming is successful, and white as well as black varieties of springbok exist.

Hunting the Springbok: Fresh Bread and Meat

The place was Omaruru, the country Namibia, and the hunt this bright August morning had been frustrated by exceptionally jittery game. The reason for this, we suspected, was that a leopard was in the region. However, we were not there to hunt leopard. We wanted a springbok. This antelope is an important meat as well as trophy animal, so we were hoping to kill two birds with one stone and get a good trophy head as well as fill the larder.

The native trackers sat now on the back of the Jeep, peering through the sharp glare of the sunlight-bathed land. The sparse winter foliage in this barren area still sufficed to give cover to the tiny steenboks that flitted in front of the Jeep like overgrown hares with horns. After a short but very jinky run, one that would make any rugby player envious, they turned and disappeared into the bush on the other side of the track. I reflected on these tiny antelope and how they live frugally on a diet of dry grass and semipoisonous and bitter plants, not even requiring water. Nature is efficient, if nothing else. Every place in the ecosystem is occupied with the appropriate plants, insects, and animals. I wondered about the human race in this respect.

I was shaken out of my contemplation when the tracker, Herman, pointed to a small herd of springbok grazing from right to left about a kilometre away. I didn't see them at first, since the whole of the countryside appeared sandy brown—the colour of springbok. I eventually could make them out with the aid of binoculars. The wind was favourable, so we got out of the Jeep and started the stalk.

Lizards regarded us with indifference from their rocky thrones as we passed by. At one place I nearly trod on a puff adder. It immediately showed a vicious side to its nature, as puff adders are prone to do, by coiling up and striking at my boot. We made a detour and left it alone.

At eighty metres I could make out a good male springbok and lay down. I sought out the shoulder, making sure that no other springbok was near or behind it, and squeezed the trigger. The stricken beast staggered and fell, beat a rapid but futile retreat with its hoofs in the air, and then lay still. The others sprung simultaneously in the air like a troupe of ballerinas and then rubber-balled it away.

As we came up to the springbok, we witnessed one of the most interesting spectacles in nature. The springbok has a pouch of skin on its back that extends to the tail. When alarmed or dying it opens this pouch and displays a white ridge of hair that acts as a visual warning. The scent in the pouch is an additional olfactory warning, and the smell reminds one of bread. With the springbok down we had the meat and could even imagine the taste of yeasty, freshly baked bread.

Waterbuck (*Kobus ellipsiprymnus*)

The common waterbuck is a relatively large and handsome animal weighing in at a maximum of three hundred kilograms and standing just under one and a half metres at the shoulder. The bulls are larger than the cows and have long, thick, ringed horns that can reach over a metre in length. Their gray hair is coarse, especially at the throat, where it forms a mane. The common waterbuck has a narrow elliptical pattern of white hair on the rump. Despite the name, the common waterbuck is also found away from water, but it does prefer to live near to it. Possibly because of its association with water and the ever-present biting insects found around water, the waterbuck has an oily secretion over its body for protection. This oily substance also pervades the meat, making it unpalatable for humans.

Hunting the Waterbuck: There is *Always* a Bigger One

We stood watching the waterbucks bounding away, showing us their ridiculous white rumps, marked like archery targets. The big buck showed us another fleeting glimpse of his long, thick-ringed horns before plunging into the reeds. Then he, too, was gone.

"That's it for today. We won't see them again. The sun'll be down in a few minutes. We can try tomorrow," my PH said.

Since these were the same words that he had said yesterday, I felt the first symptoms of waterbuck fever breaking out on my battered brow. I really wanted one of these magnificent bulls, for two reasons. First, we wanted to try for a lion and needed some bait. Although the meat from waterbuck is reputed to taste like sun cream laced with diesel oil, lions relish the stuff. Mind you, lions will eat anything. Second, I'd seen these magnificent animals in the Kruger National Park and had realized that this was a trophy that shouldn't be missing from any collection. We had seen plenty of good waterbuck here in this concession as well, but my PH had always said that there were bigger ones, with trophies like tree trunks adorning their heads. Accordingly, we had always searched further.

The next day we woke up to a dull, cloudy sky and a fine drizzle of rain that could have passed for fog. It was early winter here in Hoedspruit, Mpumalanga, South Africa, and such days can come along to change the monotony of a bright blue sky. The weather has a great influence on game as well as people. Besides temperature and wind conditions, humidity and cloud cover play an important role in determining whether game is moving or hiding.

Generally, unless you are a mad dog or an Englishman, the midday sun is avoided. Conversely, dull, cool weather with little or no wind is especially conducive to good hunting. If you add a little rain, you have a perfect hunting day. Today was no exception to this rule. We had already seen plenty of game moving along, cropping or browsing, and it was late by African standards, too. For the most part, after ten in the morning there is nothing much to do except wait for three in the afternoon. Now, at midday, we were seeing more game than ever. What's more, we saw a herd of waterbuck far out on an area of cleared scrub. Through binoculars we scanned the animals over. My PH grunted, shifted his position to better support his binoculars, and then confirmed my suspicions.

"There's a fairly good buck in that lot, but I can't tell whether it's the one we're after or not. The drizzle is making it hard to pick up much detail. Anyway, I think we should stalk over and take a better look at the goodies."

"All right," I rejoined. "Let's go and get us a waterbuck."

We started the stalk, checking the direction of the faint wind, and our tracker led us a circuitous approach. The distance narrowed to about one hundred and fifty metres, but the drizzle created a diffuse, confusing light, and we had to get nearer. We eventually got to a good place, and I shot the big bull, squarely on the shoulder, with a Silvertip bullet in .375 H&H Magnum. It dropped where it was standing. It was a very good trophy, but the measurement tape was not to be cheated; the waterbuck's horns were a shade under the minimum requirement for entry into Rowland Ward's book. I was happy enough, though, since the old bull was in superb condition and would make an excellent shoulder mount. The headskin and skull were removed with carefully whetted knives, and since we needed the meat for lion bait, nothing was going to be wasted. We loaded up the waterbuck and went to stake out the meat for the pussycats. We then drove to base camp to put the hide in salt and boil the skull.

The next day we were driving around, more interested in sightseeing than hunting. We eventually came to the place where I'd shot my slightly undersize trophy the day before. There, out in the middle of the clearing, was a massive bull waterbuck. It was not only massive; it was the grandfather of them all. It was big, proud, and arrogant-looking as it stood watching us. It turned its head this way and that, as if taunting us, showing us by how much its horns exceeded book requirements. For fun we left the Jeep and walked straight up to it; at eighty metres it was still broadside. At sixty metres it stared at us in astonishment and then started to walk off slowly. Never could we get any nearer, but I could have shot it a hundred times. My PH studied it carefully and estimated that it had horns that would place it in the top ten of Rowland Ward's book. If nothing else, hunting teaches you to be satisfied with what you've got.

Eland
(*Taurotragus oryx*)

Eland are the largest antelope in the world. There are two species: the Derby eland (*Taurotragus derbianus*), not found in South Africa, and the common eland, which is. Our present discourse is limited to the common eland. The eland has an oxlike massiveness and can reach one tonne in weight, standing a bit under two metres at the shoulder. Despite this, it can jump better than a kangaroo with its tail on fire. Standing springs of more than one and a half metres are not at all rare. Adult eland have a large dewlap at the throat. The bulls have short and thick horns, and the spiral form is well in evidence. The cows have longer and thinner horns, in which the spiral form is not so prominent. The basic body colouring of the eland is a sandy, grayish beige. A single calf is born after two hundred and sixty days of gestation. The animal is quite tractable and can be domesticated. The eland's meat is of excellent, lean quality, and the eland provides rich milk with a high fat content and twice the protein of dairy cow milk.

Hunting the Eland:
The One-Shot Method to Stop Smoking

We were hunting eland in Vaalwater, in the Northern Province of South Africa, and the weather was unseasonably warm for July. I had set my hope on getting a good bull eland, since this is a great sporting challenge. The old boys are very wary, always on the move, and can climb rocky terrain like monkeys. Also, their dull, grayish colouring melts into the background, so you can't see them. My PH, tracker, and I were now standing next to the spoor, having a drink from our water bottles. My PH had a discussion with our tracker, Andrees, and then turned to me.

"The tracks from the big bull have become mixed in with the others. He seems to have joined up with this herd of cows and calves. It's going to be difficult to follow the herd in this heat anyway, and I suggest that we take a break. The elands are going to move some more and then find shade. We can probably catch up with them in the late afternoon."

"All right. Let's find some shade and have a doze. I'm about finished by this damn heat," I replied, relieved to have a chance of respite from the energy-sapping walk. We found some shade and went off to sleep.

Three hours later we were ready to go again. Our tracker took up the spoor and we made good progress. The tracks showed that the twelve-head herd consisted of cows, calves, and a big bull. The sun was now at that annoying angle that drives spears of piercing rays directly into your eyes and makes spotting difficult. We carried on, following the dents in the sand and the ever-fresher dung from the herd. The breeze was absent this day, so we didn't have any concern about a fickle wind betraying our presence.

We were very near now. Occasionally we could catch a glimpse of a grayish patch of colour moving between the scrub and stunted trees. Our tracker went on in front of us, to try to make out where the bull was in this tangle of undergrowth and mixed herd of beasts. He went away silently, like a shadow on the ground, and we stopped and had a drink. Ten minutes later he returned and waved us onward; he whispered that he had found the big bull. Making a skirting action, we now started on a path that would intercept the elands. According to the tracker, our bull was on the left flank, and we should be able to get into position with time to spare.

Time dragged its feet now as we kneeled, waiting to see the legs of the eland bull through the bushes. I was ready to shoot, and soon my rifle started to feel heavier in my hands. Every second that passed seemed to add ten kilograms to it. Then we saw the legs of the eland. It was on a course that would bring it about one hundred metres from our present position. The bushes were thick, and I was glad that I had my .375 H&H Magnum; it needed plenty of twig-smashing power here to get to the target.

I looked through my telescopic sight and picked up the eland's legs and part of its shoulder. I followed the progress of the animal, and, when it reached a place free of vegetation, I squeezed the trigger. The slap of the bullet was music to our ears, and I knew that I'd got the bull, right on the shoulder. The other elands all stampeded away at the shot. We knew that we had to wait the time it took for a cigarette to be lit, smoked, and discarded before we could pick up the trail that led us to the bull.

Crumpled cigarette packs were removed from sweat-rimmed jackets. Even more crumpled cigarettes were removed from them, and lighter wheels were spun around, showering sparks onto gas fuel. The great ritual of the smokes was performed. Ten minutes later, after we had laced our lungs with nicotine, we set off. Andrees soon found the blood, leading off from the confusion of the other spoor. We regarded the pink and foamy lung blood and knew that we had another trophy to be proud of. This hunt had been relatively easy, not like some, in which you have to keep going and failing a thousand times before getting lucky. This hunt had been favourable from the word go: a no-problems outing that made you wish that a few more, but not all, would be like this one.

We came to a place where the bull had stopped and had let its lifeblood drip to form a miniature lake in the sand before moving on again. An animal will usually go a small distance upon being shot, but then it will stop, to watch and listen for anything that might be following. If its suspicions are not raised, it will lie down and die. On the other hand, if a wounded animal detects that something is following it, it will inject itself full of adrenaline and go as far and as fast as it can. In extreme cases you will not even find the animal. Therefore, it's always best to wait at least ten minutes (if you are a chain smoker, two cigarettes, one after the other, should suffice).

We guessed that the old boy was weakening because of blood loss. We decided to wait at this place awhile longer. We had time and enough light and the wind was right, as indicated by the smoke rising vertically from our freshly lit cigarettes. The blood was good and there was plenty of it; surely, this was the ideal situation for a hunt. The trophy was virtually in the bag, and I could almost smell the cooking of rich, red meat on the grill, mixed with the tangy scent of wood smoke. Cigarette smoke was no substitute for this, and now the butts were stamped into the sand and we proceeded.

As we came up to where it lay, the eland stared at us accusingly with large, soft bovine eyes, liquid and dark, not yet glazed with death. The glare was one of reproach. Reproach for coming here and hunting. Reproach for killing. Reproach for getting it wrong. A cow eland lay before us.

I turned away. I felt lightheaded and sick as the swoop of dismay and shame took a belt at me. This was the first time that I'd ever killed an animal by mistake. My PH stood next to me; we were both guilty of this murder. Although the blame officially was his, it had been I who had squeezed the trigger. I said nothing and walked away, leaving Andrees and my PH to field dress the eland. They went about their work quietly. The meat would be used and I would retain the trophy, although it was not from a bull. I went off and lit up a cigarette. It smelt like smouldering cardboard and tasted worse. I removed it from my mouth, threw it into the sand, and stamped it out. I'd just given up the habit. For good. Well, maybe. . . .

Steenbok
(*Raphicerus campestris*)

The diminutive steenbok is reddish fawn to grayish in colour. The belly area is white. A male adult will rarely reach fifteen kilograms in weight. Only the males carry the small black horns, which grow to about ten centimetres in length. The single young is born about two hundred days after mating.

The adaptable steenbok is found in a variety of terrain but likes lightly wooded areas and scrub land. It can climb well and can flit rapidly between and across stones and boulders. Maybe that is where it got its name, since *steenbok*, freely translated from the Afrikaans, becomes "stone buck." It is frugal and survives on grass, leaves, and any other bits of greenery it can find. It apparently does not require free water, taking liquid from the plants it eats. The steenbok is a sporting challenge but a culinary disappointment; the meat is not particularly good, being dry as a . . . stone.

Hunting the Steenbok: Will-o'-the-Wisp

Hunting is difficult and hunting steenbok is no exception. Look at it this way, the big animals present relative ease of tracking, and the target is bigger—once you get there, that is. Light will-o'-the-wisps such as steenboks leave hardly a spoor and present a difficult and small target. Add to this their habit of waiting for you to almost tread on them before bolting away like a flushed hare, and you should realize that it takes quick reactions and some luck to shoot one. Remember also, you are toting a rifle, not a shotgun. We had seen plenty of steenboks during our hunting expedition, here in Omaruru, Namibia, and, as we had filled our hunting bag with three days to spare, we decided to hunt steenbok. After all, there wasn't any pressure on us now. We only had to get a steenbok to round everything off. More easily said than done.

We set off just as the sun was burning holes in the slight morning mist and the first birds started up a tentative chirping. The Jeep contained my PH, two trackers, and yours truly. We bumped and jolted across the terrible terrain, studded with vicious thorns and spike-adorned acacia bushes. Several times we saw game, but the steenboks were not showing up today, it seemed. All the time we'd not been hunting steenbok we had seen plenty. They had even lined the way to watch us go by. They had known that we were intent on hunting anything but steenbok. Now that we were hunting them, they became scarce game. Mr. Murphy had obviously hitched a ride with us, again. Never mind, we still had plenty of time.

The day came and went and we saw virtually every species of game animal indigenous to the concession. Only steenboks were not spotted. Overnight they had achieved the population densities of woolly rhinos and mammoths. Not very high, considering that the latter have been extinct for thousands of years. Never mind, we still had two days left. A day later we had one day left, which was still plenty of time to get a steenbok.

It was nearly dark, and we were on the way home. We were minding a lot because we were empty-handed. The steenboks had beaten us because this *was* the end of the hunt. We had tried everything, but time, luck, patience, money, and liquor had run out on us all at once. It is at times like these when you have to assess the whole hunt in context and not let the failure to obtain a certain species cloud the day. Anyway, you can ask yourself, who in his right mind wants a tiny, sneaky steenbok? You tell yourself that you've got oryx, springbok, and a marvelous mountain zebra, and a whole lot of other trophies, and you don't even have place for a steenbok trophy back home. You relive the other moments of the chase, the stalks, the crawls, the tracks, and the shots. You don't register the jolts of the Jeep as it pulls you toward the base camp and, inexorably, the end of the hunt. You start thinking about how the trophies will be prepared, because, in their present boiled-skull and salt-encrusted state, it seems that they will never take the form of the animal they once were. No taxidermist could ever do them enough justice. You hope that you are wrong.

The Jeep stops, and the trackers are pointing out to a small, brownish pucklike animal under some scrub. You jump out of the Jeep and follow a tracker; he points. You shoot, and it lies there, dead. You've shot a steenbok, at last. Even though time was short, it had still been more than enough to get a will-o'-the-wisp.

Zebra
(*Equus zebra*)

First, a bit of background about Africa's striped horses before we start hunting them. Let's get this clear from the start: I like zebras. A lot. To me they symbolize the wildness of Africa. They cannot be tamed and saddled or yoked to pull a plough. They are a characteristic part of Africa's fauna, and *everybody* knows what they are. Or do they? Many do not realize that there are several species of zebra. A casual glance puts them all into the category of black-and-white striped horses, but a closer look at their size, habitats, and stripe patterns will indicate differences. Like fingerprints, no two stripe patterns in a given species are the same.

Zebras are related to horses, and they too are grass croppers. Zebras live about twenty years, and the gestation time is around a year and a month. In common with horses, they can bite, kick, and run hard; they have to—the lions, you know. The quagga (*Equus quagga*) is extinct. Formerly, this species was common in southern Africa, but it was extirpated in the late 1870s. It was characterized by a sparsely striped lower body.

Grevy zebra (*Equus grevyi*) is an endangered species. This is the largest and most handsome of all wild horses, weighing up to four hundred and fifty kilograms. It has a narrow black-and-white pattern except for the belly, which is white. It lives in subdesert areas in Ethiopia and Kenya. It was first displayed in Rome in 3 B.C. as a "tiger horse." Maybe those old Romans were colour-blind.

Burchell zebra (*Equus burchelli*) are still common but have declined in number generally because of competition from domestic livestock. The stallions fight viciously for the mares and serious injuries can occur. The animals weigh up to about three hundred and eighty kilograms. They are found in a wide variety of habitats but must have water daily. Too bad the lions know this as well.

The Hartmann mountain zebra (*Equus zebra hartmannae*), as its name would imply, is found up in the mountains. It occurs in two varieties: one in South Africa and one in Namibia and Angola. The mountain zebras have a small dewlap at their throat. They are the smallest zebras, weighing in at about three hundred kilograms.

You see, there is a bit more to zebras than white stripes on a black background. Or is it the other way around? No matter, let's go hunting. The following describes what happened when I hunted Burchell zebra and Hartmann mountain zebra.

Hunting the Burchell Zebra: Lend Me Your Ears

The sun was crawling its way determinedly up the sky as we set off on foot to reduce the number of Burchell zebra by two. It was July and winter, and we were on the Vaalwater property, north of Johannesburg, South Africa. The veld was in very bad shape because of the lack of rain and overgrazing. The landowner had made a count of his zebra and had decided to shoot out a couple of old stallions to lessen the fighting and to give some younger ones a chance at breeding. I turned to my PH.

"So, the zebras have been fighting. Tell me about it, and we'll see how we can stop them."

"Yes. The two old stallions that we are after have been going at it hammer and tongs. They've been kicking and biting the hell out of each other. Something to do with the ladies, as usual. Another thing is that the zebras are close-cropping the only bit of grass left on the veld. The owner will soon have to start scattering lucerne to augment the fodder. He told me that if you shoot out the two stallions, the trophy fees will more than cover the cost for fodder. It's therefore a good time to kill two birds with one stone—or should I say two zebras? Anyway, I reckon that you'll need more than one stone, er, I mean bullet," he added facetiously.

"Look here, if you gave him the daily fee that I am paying you he could buy a new property complete with lush grass," I retorted. "You know that I've sighted in with the .308 and it was all right. You're only mad because I shot more tens on the paper target than you did. Now stop moaning and lead me to these striped donkeys."

"It's not that easy, my friend. Zebras can hear, see, and even smell a leaf falling off a tree. You'll see that those two old boys will give you a lot of stick. They didn't get old by being stupid," he added.

"Funny, you did!" I rapped back, only just avoiding a thump.

We followed our tracker, whose name was Tea. He got his name because he doubled as a camp helper and brought us tea every morning with a greeting of, "Tea." He lifted up his hand and pointed to a patch of scrub. I focused my binoculars on the place but could see nothing at first. Then patterns of black-and-white stripes slowly appeared, like a photograph in the developing bath, superimposed on the black sticks and twigs. The zebras were in front of us, and their camouflage was perfect. We were about two hundred metres away. I wanted to get in much closer, not being too sure about the knockdown power of the .308 calibre compared with my usual .375 H&H Magnum. I had borrowed the .308 because I'd run out of cartridges for the big rifle.

A herd of about eight zebras was standing in a sun-dappled clearing. Occasionally we caught a glimpse of a tail swished or a head shaken to dislodge the flies, and all the time we crept in closer. The stallions were nowhere to be seen. We got to within eighty or so metres and then glassed them over again. It is difficult to determine the sex of a zebra at this distance. We could make out a few mares, since they had foals by them, but there was no sign of any stallion. The wind was favourable to our intention and we had not yet been seen.

My PH turned to me.

"Are you ready?" he whispered. "If so, we can stand up and let the zebras see us. The effect will be, according to theory, that they will clear off."

I looked at him, now having had my suspicions confirmed as to his mental condition.

"That's a theory if ever I heard one! Of course they will clear off, man! I mean, we've just spent the morning being cooked to the consistency of frizzled bacon by the sun, and we get up this close and then we jump up and, surprisingly, they run off. A truly *brilliant* way to hunt. Are you out of your mind? Don't bother answering, I know the answer."

"Don't worry, my friend. The zebras that we don't want will run off, but the stallion we do want will not. The stallion always waits a bit longer before he loses his nerve and follows the rest. You'll see. Get ready for quick shooting, when I say."

I cast him a long-suffering look and got ready, despite my utter disbelief. We stood up and, no surprise, the zebras ran away. In less than five seconds it was all over. I stood tensed, squinting my eyes through the glare and the dust, ready to snap off a shot should the stallion appear. It didn't. We waited some more. It did, about a minute later. I held the cross hairs on the place on the shoulder, swung forward, and squeezed the trigger. The bullet slap came to us, but the zebra made no sign that it had been shot. Five minutes later we took up the blood spoor. There was plenty of sign, and we could follow it to where the stallion lay.

He was thrashing about on the ground, moribund, only just alive. Down but not yet out. His eyes rolled white in his skull. He was champing his spittle and blood-flecked jowls, tasting the salty-coppery flavour of blood in his mouth and chewing at the bloodied grass for a frenzied last meal. He was real mean, and you could tell that he hated us for killing him in this way. It's at times like these when extra caution is required. Zebras are capable of undergoing a Jekyll and Hyde transformation when wounded. They have a mouth crammed full with blunt but large yellowish green teeth that are capable of grinding and tearing large pieces out of anything unfortunate enough to get between them. A zebra's bite is definitely worse than its bray. The immense pressure of the bite will cause excruciating pain over the area that our striped friend has latched on to. You'll also be amazed at the colour of the Victoria plum bruising it will raise. You can get a fair idea of a zebra's bite by inserting your thumb into the jamb of a door and then getting someone to slam the door closed. Right? A zebra's arsenal doesn't finish with its teeth, either. You have to add four hoofs and a kick that will fracture your skull to the consistency of a shattered coconut. You see, the gentle-looking zebra is a nasty fighting machine that you may have to deal with if you don't shoot straight.

Remembering all this and keeping clear of the flailing hoofs and champing teeth, I placed an insurance shot into the zebra's shoulder. As it died the zebra lost control of its anal sphincter muscle, and vast amounts of green excrement plopped out of its bowels. A stream of clear semen also started to dribble out of its shriveled black penis to mix with the blood on the sand. It was a paradox; the solids and liquids of life were now the effluents of death. Do men also go through this show of babyhood, requiring diapers for incontinence, at the very end?

My PH stooped down, pulled the zebra's rubbery lips to one side, and examined its teeth. It now sneered at us about its own death. That's one hell of a sense of humour! The flat greenish yellow chisels were worn, and darker dentine showed through. The cutting surfaces were flat but still quite capable of cropping grass, or your finger. My PH looked up.

"Well now, I told you that you'd need more than one bullet, didn't I? Anyway, you've got a good old stallion here. The teeth are worn, and look, he's got no ears."

I now noticed that the zebra was lacking both ears. They looked like the chewed-up cauliflower ears of a professional boxer. This old fighter had lost his ears in the process of sorting out his rivals. Or their sorting him out. I had intended to have a full shoulder mount, but a zebra without ears is not a pretty sight. I looked at the fallen prizefighter again, noting his worn-down, rounded-off hoofs, bitten ears and scars, cuts and bald patches. Mine was a very ugly zebra, indeed. I turned to my PH.

"I think that we should take only the skin and not worry about a cape. The other stallion might be a bit more presentable than this one."

My PH went back to get the Jeep, and Tea started surgery. A knife was inserted and stroked gently along the tight-as-a-drumskin belly. Bowels bulged blue gray through the belly lining, and slowly the pinstriped suit was peeled off the zebra. Lumps of bright yellow fat hung in its paunch, and Tea collected the tallow for reasons best known to himself. I suspected, though, that it was to be used much as lion fat is.

We field dressed the carcass and threw the slabs of slobbery, dark red, coarse-grained meat into the back of the Jeep. Fresh zebra meat is not very fine in texture or flavour, but it makes passable biltong, that air-cured specialty of South Africa. The viscera were left on the veldt for the hyenas. It would all be gone by tomorrow. The skin was covered in salt and rolled up, and we went back to base. It was late; tomorrow we would try for the other zebra.

The next day we got up early, and we had found the herd of zebras by nine o'clock. We guessed that the other stallion would not be far away, and, noticing the absence of his old sparring partner, would have quickly joined up with the ladies. He had done just that. The stalk went well, the .308 worked well, and the stallion was shot well. It died running, and death had frozen its gallop. Its ears were also chewed, and its neck was bitten to pieces. Scars marred the pattern all over its battered body. It had obviously taken as much leather as the other stallion. Again we took only the skin and meat, since I had given up the wish for a shoulder mount. In retrospect, I reckon that old zebra stallions are so pugilistic that you'll never get a good one in fair condition. Just shows you what fighting over ladies can do.

Hunting the Mountain Zebra: Trouble with Wind

This marks the end of the plains game part of this book. The mountain zebra is here not for alphabetical reasons, nor because it was the last species I shot; it wasn't. Actually, it was the very first animal that I hunted in Africa.

It was the first day of the hunt near to Omaruru, Namibia. It was my first time in Africa as well, and it was August: ideal for hunting, since the normally sparse vegetation is even sparser. Despite a vicious pummeling from the hard wood of the rifle butt (the weapon was new and I didn't yet have a rubber shock absorber attached), I had sighted in accurately to 180 metres with 300-grain conical-point bullets in calibre .375 H&H Magnum. As a greenhorn to African hunting, I had still a lot to learn about hunting, bullets, and recoil.

My PH was the owner of the property. Now we were bouncing along a rough track in his Jeep. Two black trackers were with us. The going was slow, since the sharp-toothed rocks were waiting like grinning sharks to open up the Jeep's underside and then feed on its guts. It needed only a lack of concentration and the oil pan would be punctured and we'd be walking home. We approached the more mountainous part of the 25,000-hectare property and stopped to view the area.

We made out a lone zebra high up on a plateau. Lone animals are usually very old stallions. Getting out of the Jeep we started a circuitous approach and, within half an hour, we were within range. We wanted an old, broken-down stallion, and we could now see that the one standing broadside to us was going to satisfy this glue factory criterion. I had confidence in the rifle, and the 150 metres to the zebra seemed closer through the telescopic sights. I sought out a particular white stripe on the shoulder and squeezed the trigger. The bullet made a soggy-wet *shplock* sound, and the zebra reared high. It paddled its forelegs in the air before thundering off into the rocky cover. We stood watching the place, and silence crept back slowly as the rifle fire echoed itself to death in the hills. The question was whether the zebra had been shot to death. It had. However, the treacherous cone-point bullet had disintegrated on the outside of the zebra, and there was virtually no penetration to the vital organs. The small splinter of copper that had just made it to the inside had only nicked the lung. From that day, I used only Silvertip bullets.

We took some photographs and then skinned and field dressed the zebra. We slung the slabs of meat on the back of the Jeep and drove away. When we got back to base, about twenty native dogs of dubious and motley origins ran out to greet us, barking joyfully. Their mood didn't last long, and snarling and fang-vicious dogfights soon broke out as they jockeyed for position to secure a piece of the meat. We brought the best pieces to the cold room and left lumps of fatty meat and gristle for the canines to clear. This was a mistake, because the dogs were waiting for us the next morning, expecting another feed. That in itself was not bad, but, when dogs have eaten raw zebra meat, they become prone to severe attacks of wind. The broken wind (and there is plenty of it) stinks worse than rotten eggs. This is supportable if the dogs keep away from you. Unfortunately, the camp dogs had now accepted us into their pack, as the main meat suppliers, I suppose, and insisted on keeping us company. As we set off on foot for the hunt, they led us, coming far out into the hunting concession with us. This was serious—not so much because of the barking but because we were downwind from our fearsomely flatulent four-legged friends. (I hope that my attempt at poetic alliteration gives you a feeling for what it's like to be near a pack of dogs with zebra-meat-induced flatulence—if not the smell.)

Chapter 8

Birds: Guinea Fowl and Sandgrouse

Bird hunting (or should I say shooting?) can be every bit as challenging and rewarding as plains game or Big Five hunting; it is certainly cheaper. The variety of game birds in Africa is almost endless. The doves, francolins, sand grouse, guinea fowl, and geese all make for good sport. If the shotgunner is using the right size shot, leading the birds enough with his shotgun, and not shooting too far—or too near—he may be able to richly supplement his diet. After all, too much steak is not good for you.

It saddens me to see the product of guinea fowl (*Numida mitrata*) domestication stretched out on the poultry dealer's slab. The anemic white skin, dotted all over with pale pimples, and the knowledge that this is a bird that has hardly flown in all its sterile and short life are enough to ruin one's appetite. The real McCoy has dark meat of exquisite flavour. Guineas are ugly birds with funereally drab, blackish gray feathers and a heavy sprinkling of white measles spots. Their heads are naked, blue-and-red, and vulturelike. The top of the head is adorned with a helmet of hard bone, like a shark's fin, giving it its other name, helmeted guinea fowl. They have two blue-and-red-tipped flaps of skin hanging down their cheeks like solidified tears of ice. Quite a rough-looking bird, but the proof of the pudding is in the eating. This applies very much so to guineas. They have excellent meat, and, when you sink your teeth into a suitably roasted one, well now, you can forgive it for being so ugly. Almost. The old birds are a bit tough if they've had a lot of flying time under their wings and are cooked improperly. However, even a tough guinea fowl, or *tarantaal*, as it is known in South Africa, is a very good piece of eating. Now, pour yourself a drink; red or white wine will be just fine for the guinea fowl that are up next on the menu.

Shooting Helmeted Guinea Fowl: The Attack of the Tarantaals

A moment comes in every hunt when the serious things have been achieved or you've given up or the time has nearly run out or the liquor has. Or all. If you do happen to have a bit of time before leaving the bush, then it is worthwhile doing some bird shooting. You'll need a shotgun and plenty of shells and you're in business. We knew guinea fowl were wreaking havoc on a farm near the Blyde River, Mpumalanga, South Africa, because the farmer had called us up to ask if we could help reduce their numbers. We told him we could. We did.

The next day my PH and I were waiting for the guinea fowls to fly in from their roosts and to land on a newly planted wheat field. As the sun rose, the pheasant-sized birds started to fall out of the sky by the hundreds. They came over in seemingly never-ending flocks and, banking steeply, descended like gray blue balls of feather onto the field, where they started immediately to pick out the grain.

We let the birds come in and soon the field became black with them, all picking and hacking away rhythmically. It was time to move. Since the inherently suspicious birds have excellent eyesight, it was no use to try to approach them slowly across the flat field. It was also no use trying to get at them from the other side of the field, which was bordered with bushes, because they were in the middle: too far away even for the fifty-gram loads of four-millimetre-diameter shot from our magnum scatterguns. The tactic we thought out was the direct approach. Checking our shotguns, we stepped out and made a brisk walk to where our feathered friends were feeding and frolicking. Some continued feeding, but a few stopped frolicking and looked at us distrustfully. Several became agitated, and a few hundred started to increase the distance between us and them. We quickened our pace. The birds did likewise. Some were soon going full speed, heads level with the ground, like feathered racing cars with the turbo booster at full tilt. The more fainthearted of the flock were already bumping along like novice pilots, partly flying, partly running. A few downright cowards had already taken to the air.

We had lessened the distance to about sixty metres when the birds collectively assumed the worse about the business at hand and lifted off. They blotted out the sun as they banked and flew over us. We opened up on them. *Boom boom, boom boom*. Eject, shove in two more shells. *Boom boom, boom boom*, eject. We unleashed our swarms of copper-plated steel hornets and heard the sharp *zish brup, zish brup* sound of steel pellets contacting feathers as we knocked them from out of the sky. We continued to pepper them with shot, but it was quickly over before the final shell was discharged at the last and fast-disappearing bird. We had emptied the field except for the eleven guineas now lying there.

We collected our spent shell cases and went over to the birds. A couple still flapped weakly, making necessary a pull of their necks. The fluttering stopped. We picked up our bounty and left the area, moving about three kilometres down the road to the other field. The guineas had landed there and were busy pecking at the farmer's wheat again, driving him to financial ruin. We repeated our trick, deftly dusting them over, and we got five more birds. We waited about an hour to let things settle down and went back to our original place.

They were there, but this time they didn't even wait for us to get within a hundred metres and made a scramble fit to shame any air force in the world. They turned, and the squadrons flew over us at about the speed of sound and a mile high. Too fast and high to shoot. We stood staring at them, faces upturned, and then the first "missiles" hit us. The cheeky beggars were mounting a counterattack and had flown over to lay down organic "chemical bombs" on us. They scored one direct hit on the head of my PH and a shoulder and chest hit on me. We cleaned off the droppings but reckoned that we had won, in any case. We left the battlefield and went home.

We ate well. I had a couple roasted. I even had one stuffed. Not as in culinary stuffing, but as in taxidermy. The taxidermist did a great job. I now have a guinea fowl on my worktable, from where it regards me with a bright, glassy eye and a questioning cock of its head. In time, I even got to think that guinea fowl were pretty—pretty ugly. And I shall never forget that they are prone to foul play.

(PS. The fieldfare, a thrushlike bird of Europe, also uses droppings to attack enemies near its nesting sites. The excrement is jettisoned with deadly accuracy and can ruin a predator bird's feathers, thus preventing it from flying for a while. Maybe the guineas learnt their bomb-dropping tactics from them; the beggars certainly were accurate enough on us!)

Shooting the Sand Grouse: Fast-Flying Fun

Thank goodness that bird-shooting possibilities in Africa are not limited to those ugly guinea fowl. Try sand grouse, as an alternative; they are most challenging birds to shoot. The first stage in converting a few of these fast-flying balls of feather into a delicious meal is to get up very early in the morning and wait in good cover for the squadrons to fly over the watering holes. They come quickly, when daylight has just banished the night. One moment the big, blue sky is empty; the next moment you hear the strident peeping sound of your quarry as they approach strongly and directly on rapidly beating long and pointed wings. They are spread out in a typical V formation to avoid the turbulence generated by the other flyers. Suddenly they are there, banking and folding down their wings, stabbing at the air to brake and lose height. Suddenly you are firing at them. And missing. They wheel around and pick up speed and are gone. Maybe three seconds have passed. You stand there with your shotgun barrels belching smoke like double Havana cigars. Birds one, hunter nil.

You quickly rerun the video tape of the action in your mind's eye and do a bit of calculation. Yes, you were leading nicely. By the time your brain had given your trigger finger the command to squeeze, and by the time the shot had been ejected from the barrel and had traveled in the direction of the birds, it was already too late. The birds had been at least five metres out of the swarm of steel pellets you'd sent them. Well, you say, you'll lead the next lot even more. The next ones come and you lead them more. You miss them all. Now is the time when you become disheartened. The procedure is repeated and by the time your box of twenty-five shot shells has run down to a remnant of six you have only one small sand grouse at your feet. Not a great feat, merely enough to grouse about! This individual bird had

had an unlucky day, being foolish enough to intercept a stray pellet.

The sun is rising quickly now, and you know that the morning's flight of sand grouse will soon be over. Another formation comes in. It's now or never. You throw the shotgun to your shoulder. Forget all about lead theory and shoot much too far ahead of the birds. You are amazed to see the V pattern disintegrate as four birds tumble, with a puff of feathers, from out of the formation. They crash untidily onto the ground, and, as you pick up the last one, you note a few feathers still drifting down from out of the sky. So, you got lucky at last. Enough for today. You pick up the spent shells and feel a bit guilty that your shooting average is four shot shells per bird. You make a mental note to buy shares in the shot shell manufacturer's company. With a turnover like the present one it must be an undiscovered blue-chip possibility.

You take a look at your birds, noting their soft and shining brown feathers and delicate black markings. You note the short, feathered pinky legs and toes, the rufus brown head, blackish stripes, nicely pointed tail, and the beak adapted for seed eating. Altogether a much prettier bird than a guinea fowl.

Chapter 9

Snake Trilogy: Black Mamba

Let's now forget the game animals that can get you your death certificate, your ticket to Tombstone. Africa is bristling with plenty of other baddies. You see, Africa is home sweet home to a great variety of reptiles, spiders, insects, and plants that are potentially deadly or, at the least, can cause unpleasant reactions when they get into intimate contact with your skin or try to tap a vein. Poisoning or envenomation depends on the noxious substance getting into your bloodstream, and Mother Nature, bless her soul, has been particularly inventive in providing the means to achieve this. Examples are the sharp hairs on stinging nettles, stings in the tails of assorted insects, and, of course, the hollow teeth of snakes, which are the world's original hypodermic needles.

The next three chapters deal with the never-ending battle between humans and snakes. Ever since the Garden of Eden there has been a special love or hate relationship between us and them. In my opinion all snakes are best avoided, since some species have the very antisocial habit of killing people. The list of snakes capable of seriously disrupting your hunting plans or even preventing you from collecting your pension is quite long, as we shall find out.

Trouble with Tamboti and Mamba

We had filled our safari bag in the Vaalwater concession in South Africa, taking a few trophy heads. The skulls had been boiled clean and the capes were drying in the sun, covered with a thick layer of salt. This moment, which comes in every hunt, is a bittersweet one, making the hunter happy and sad at the same time. Your purpose for coming to this far land was to hunt and experience the African adventure. Lady Luck was with you, at least some of the time, and you have been more or less successful. You now have a day or two in which you have little to do except shoot at paper targets, relax, and smoke (unless you've just kicked the habit again). Surely this is ideal. Wrong. The clock ticks for everyone, and every second brings you closer to the moment when you must leave and return to the concrete jungle, back home. We had exhausted our rations. Now the opportunity to hunt for some meat came as a welcome distraction to the depressing sight of our black helpers packing up our things, ready for transport to the airport.

Our tracker spotted the group of bachelor impala rams, sheltering from the midday heat under the thick thornbushes. Making out a suitable individual, I decided to convert him into venison stew and started the stalk, getting into a position to shoot. The distance was only about fifty metres, but the nature of the thick thornbushes made the shot difficult. I was using a rifle in calibre Winchester .243, since a fast and light flat-shooting bullet with a soft nose is adequate for the thin-skinned impala at such distances. A fast and light bullet is not, however, ideal for shooting through heavy tangles of bush. This fact would soon become evident.

Lying on the ground, I waited for the ram to move into a more open position. Time ground on, and the sun beat down on me, raising sweat on my brow that trickled into my eyes, irritating them. At last, the ram moved to the left and stood broadside to me; I snicked off the safety and placed the cross hairs of the telescopic sight a touch behind his shoulder and squeezed the trigger. The rifle went off, a small piece of lead left the barrel at high speed, and all the impalas vanished, it seemed, even more quickly.

We waited ten minutes and went to the place. Peacock, our black tracker, scouted around, muttering to himself, and then stopped, like a pointer dog before a pheasant. He called us over to show the places where my bullet had broken a few twigs in passing and had been deflected. Not good. Peacock then pointed to the small spot of blood on a stone that was reflecting the sun's rays. Even worse. Damn, we had a wounded animal! This at the end of a safari in which everything had, until now, gone so well.

We took up the hunt, allowing Peacock to unravel our animal's spoor from the myriad hoofprints on the ground. We followed him and noted here and there a spot of blood on a blade of grass or dripped onto a stone. We followed him up hill and down dale. We followed him across a small, dried-up riverbed, and always there was that tiny red sign. The ram had gone into thicker bush. We stopped and took out our water bottles. It was looking bad, because we'd been on the spoor for an hour now. A glance at the sun told us that we had four hours before night. We followed Peacock. The blood spoor had nearly stopped by now, and it was a marvel to see our tracker still following the animal even though it was mixed in with a lot of other spoor.

Suddenly, Peacock squeaked and jumped back, almost knocking my PH over, on top of me. Disentangling ourselves, we looked around to see what the cause was for his alacrity in making the change from vanguard to rearguard. A sharp hissing sound as from a punctured tyre came from just in front of us, and we stepped back, searching the grass and bushes for what we knew was there. It lay, scaly and brown, coiled on a boulder, regarding us with a no-nonsense malevolent glitter in its eyes. Its tongue flickered in and out of its mouth like strokes of black forked lightning, waving up and down, testing the air for our scent. We retreated to watch one of the most dangerous snakes in the world, certainly Africa, uncoil and slither down the side of the boulder in one liquid movement and away into the grass. The black mamba (*Dendroaspis polylepis*) is a very bad *noga.* It is the most feared snake on the African continent because its bite usually causes death—as in final curtains, funerals, and R.I.P. (Reptile Intensive Poisoning.)

The name "black mamba" is misleading, because this snake with the big poison sacs filled to the brim with venom is actually gray or dull olive brown in colour. The name really describes the colour of the inside of the mouth, and, believe me, the snake has a tendency to open its mouth on the slightest provocation. The story goes this way: The longer the mamba, the shorter its temper. Just imagine, if you will, a short temper that goes up to four metres long. I've seen a mamba virtually swim through the tops of chest-high grass; I estimated that it could have overtaken a running person with ease. The snake is characterized by an aggressive nature and a tendency to come after you, and quickly, if it feels threatened or if you have been unfortunate enough to get between it and its hidey hole. Once it has caught up with you, it is not shy about giving you a big, toothy kiss, either. Couple this trait with one of the most potent snake venoms known (it is a cocktail of complex chemicals each of which synergistically boosts the nasty effects of the others), and you see why clever people, like you and me, run away when they see a mamba.

The overall toxic effect of a snakebite will depend on many factors, such as the species of snake, the place it bit, the quantity of venom injected, the person's constitution, how quickly the spread of the poison could be stopped, and whether antivenin was quickly available. A big dose of mamba venom in the region of your throat will work more rapidly than a slight nip on the end of your finger—if for no other reason than the problem of applying the tourniquet. ("What bad luck. He would have survived the snake bite, but the tourniquet strangled him!") Bad news: Mamba bites are most often on the top half of the body, because of the length of the snake. Whether or not antivenin is used depends on if you are allergic to the stuff. A sensitivity test must first be done; otherwise, the reaction to the antidote could itself be fatal. Die from snakebite or from the cure. It's your choice. A disgustingly healthy individual will stand a better chance of surviving the shock, pain, and poisonous effects of the bite than will someone just recovering from malaria, influenza, a heart attack, or a recent visit to the Inland Revenue Office.

The venom of snakes is modified saliva. It is a complex mixture of proteins and polypeptides that have both toxic and enzymatic effects. The primary purpose of the venom is to aid digestion of the prey. It also immobilizes the prey and serves as a defense when the snake is directly attacked or accidentally trodden on. Venom must be quick acting and cause the prey to lose its ability to run away. Therefore a high degree of paralysis is required from the venom cocktail. The knockout may be achieved by affecting the muscles or the heart and respiratory functions. In any case, a mamba bite will act quickly to cause the recipient of its mandibular attentions to lose the ability to walk, talk, swallow, and move the eyes, tongue, and lower jaw. Add to this a progressive slowing down of the rate of breathing and a massive decrease in blood pressure, plus the necessity for artificial respiration, and you should get the picture of how serious a bite from this particular *noga* is. There doesn't seem to be much pain from a mamba bite. This is fairly typical for a nerve poison, or neurotoxin.

Our fanged friends, the mambas (there are four species), have fixed venom fangs in their jaw. They are classed as proteroglyph, and the fangs are relatively short (6 millimetres, or a quarter of an inch). In contrast, the puff adder (*Bitis arietans*) and Gabon viper (*Bitis gabonica*) have venom fangs that fold into their mouths like the blade of a penknife; they can be flicked into action when necessary. They are classed as solenoglyph. These teeth may reach 25 millimetres (an inch) or more in length. Mambas are oviparous (egg-laying) snakes. Usually, up to fourteen elongated eggs are laid at the start of the rainy season. Mambas are quite active during the day, and, although rare, a meeting with one is never much of a pleasure. My personal assessment is that if your confrontation has got so far as playing dentist with a mamba (or any other snake, for that matter), it's high time to be running the opposite way.

After having made sure that the mamba had left, we went on farther into the bush. We soon found the impala. The bullet had fragmented on a twig and had sent a splinter of lead into its neck, causing the loss of blood. We had to wonder, though, because the amount of blood on the spoor had been only slight and seemed hardly enough to cause death. We gutted the impala, leaving the insides for the jackals and hyenas, and carried it back to camp. It was dark before we saw the tiny ruby spot of the campfire. We knew that we had been lucky to have come away unscathed in our brush with a mamba. We'd been even luckier to have found the impala, because we all had one hell of a gnawing hunger. Back in camp, we took out the filets and placed them on a griddle over the fire. The meat was not hung or ripened, but as it came from a young animal, it promised to be tender.

Whilst watching the blue and yellow flames licking the wood, a wave of nausea suddenly hit me with a swoop, the way it does in the Big Dipper at the fair. Sweat beaded my brow, and I felt terrible. If it's possible to feel colour, then I felt lime-green. I stood up and called to my PH. He had been busy packing out some things and had not yet been near to the cooking fire. As he approached, I saw his face contort with anger as he went over to the fire and started kicking sand into it. One of the camp helpers, who went by the ridiculous name of Comfort, had put logs of very poisonous tamboti wood on the fire, and this was emitting the noxious smoke and making me feel as if I had a cognac hangover. Comfort was told, very clearly, to improve his knowledge of poisonous plants. It took me a while to recover. Later on, washing the impala steaks down with wine (the filets had been ruined by the smoke), we discussed the events of the day. I still couldn't believe that the impala had died as a result of the slight wound it had received. My PH agreed.

"The bullet wound was too slight. Maybe that mamba had something to do with it."

I asked him what he was driving at.

"Just imagine that the impala had passed too near to the mamba, and the snake had struck out and had bitten it. Mambas have the tendency to bite anything near to them. I once found a dead kudu near a mamba hole. It had been bitten, and the hole still contained the mamba, which hissed like a steam engine if you got near. It was probably a female with eggs. Anyway, in the present case, the shock from the bullet wound, the loss of blood, plus the bite might have been just enough together. That mamba seemed reluctant to launch an attack on us, maybe because of its depleted reserves of venom. It is a plausible explanation, at least."

"Well," I commented, "I'll buy that, but, if that's the case, the steaks that we've just eaten have been marinated with premium-grade, lead-free, high-octane mamba juice!"

"I never thought about it like that, but yes," he replied. "You could have a point there. Never mind, since you like your steaks well done, the heat of the fire has probably destroyed the mamba poison."

I felt the bile rise again. The thought of eating mamba poison, neutralized or not, was not balm to a stomach recovering from tamboti toxins. That's Africa for you, if the mamba doesn't get you, the tamboti will. For good measure, the mamba had come around for a second time and put the finishing touch on another perfect day.

Can of Worms

It was the end of a day's hunting that had resulted in nothing. Sure, we had seen plenty of animals, but not the sort that we were looking for, because Mr. Murphy was still with us. Now, whisky glasses in hand, reflecting the flickering flames of the new (nonpoisonous) campfire, we sat waiting for the cook to announce dinner. At times like this, it is just good to relax and think over the day or tell a joke or two. It's also a good time to relate "Bushy tales." My PH leaned forward, pushed a twig into the fire, and started his tale.

"I knew a farmer up in Zimbabwe who had plenty of trouble with cattle just dying on him. He used to find piles of 'em dead, near to the watering point, and didn't know what the hell was going on. They found out, eventually, that the main path to the water passed near to a hole in which a big mamba had made its home. Mambas like their peace and quiet and hate visitors. Come to think about it, they just about hate the guts of bloody anything. This one had therefore taken to the habit of biting anything that passed close by, the result of which was plenty of dead cattle. It was decided to kill the snake. The next day a few spectators had assembled to see how the business would go. The three-strong labour force became increasingly unsure as they approached the hole slowly, with their spades held in front of them for protection. The farmer stood to the side, his shotgun filled with buckshot.

Judging by the hissing sound coming from the hole, the mamba was getting highly agitated and definitely not in agreement with the terms of its forthcoming execution. Anyway, the mamba shot out of its hole like a greased javelin, only to disappear into an adjacent one. The attentions of the diggers now turned to the new residence. A careful approach by the executioners ended in a chaotic scramble as they bolted like frightened rabbits away from the snake as it vacated the hole and went back into its former abode. The intrepid snake killers were getting nowhere, but the mamba was getting angry. At this rate, the next thing would be that someone would be bitten. Bites from mambas, rest assured (or should I say, rest in peace), are not good for your health.

An old blackman who had been watching the action now came forward and suggested that he knew how to drive mambas permanently from their residences. All you need, he said, was to prepare a thick porridge of cattle dung and water and to pour the green mess down into the hole. A suitable mixture was duly made up in an old tin. Much arguing took place concerning who would have the dubious honour of pouring the pungent poultice into the mamba's residence, but eventually they managed to mob a suitable idiot into the suicide mission.

The intrepid dung delivery man now stood near the hole and started to dribble the pungent potion down into it. A hissing sound like the noise of a gushing geyser erupted from the bowels of the earth, as the magic mixture made contact. The man slammed the tin over the hole just in time to contain the snake and beat a hasty retreat. Now, that's a can of worms! They waited half an hour, and the farmer decided to shoot the tin off the hole. Unfortunately for the mamba, it was residing under the tin, trying no doubt to avoid the soup of the day. It got a good peppering of shot and died in a writhing mess of coils. Just how much the dose of dung contributed to the success of the mission, I don't know. C'mon, Popeye! Let's go and have dinner. I believe we have pureed spinach, tonight!"

Chapter 10

Snake Trilogy: Spitting Cobra

In Vaalwater, in the Northern Province of South Africa, winter starts about May and ends in October. Winter is a good hunting season because, at this time, the vegetation vanishes and visibility increases. The masses of leaves that had limited your view to a few metres are now thinner, and the bare twigs of the bushveld afford less cover to the game. Of course, the game can also better see the approaching hunter. The mornings are as cold as the evenings, sometimes touching the freezing point, and biting winds now barge roughly through the bare boughs of the fever and *marula* trees. The sky is mostly clear and blue, and midday temperatures can reach around 20 degrees centigrade. One advantage of all this is that there are fewer biting insects around and, thankfully, hardly any snakes. There are, however, exceptions to the rule.

Snakes are reptiles, and as such they rely on their surroundings for their body heat. When it gets colder they become torpid, and they search out dark places in the ground or in hollow trees and wait for warmer days. During a normal winter hunt one will rarely see a snake. It's just too cold for them. Mother Nature being what she is, there are those capricious days in early winter that exceed the temperatures of midsummer. Believe me, snakes really appreciate this and come out to soak up the heat and to lie in your way. Too bad.

We had been hunting and had celebrated our success until the early morning hours. Consequently, we were ill disposed to get up from bed and had decided to have a lie-in and hunt in the afternoon. After all, I was supposed to be on holiday as well as hunting. It was a freak hot spell, and it would be a bit cooler at the end of the day. When I woke up, the sun was high in the sky.

I lay abed a while, sweating in my tent. Listening to the clank of saucepans as the midday meal was being prepared, I got up and, putting on my glasses, shuffled my way over to the washbasin. Suddenly, a fine spray of liquid covered my face and glasses. The malevolent hissing sound that followed snapped me out of my drowsiness. My eyes focused through the venom-spattered lenses to pick out a fair representative of the Mozambique spitting cobra (*Naja mossambica*) family coiled up in the corner of the tent.

As it reared up, I fell backward and over the edge of the bed. I scrambled to the other side and shouted the good news that a visitor had got into my tent. Within seconds I could see the shapes of the black helpers silhouetted against the canvas. After inquiring what was wrong, and having been told that a Mozambique spitting cobra had decided to move in with me, one of them answered in muffled tones, from the outside:

"Eeh, dis t'ing, he *plenty* bad news, Suh. You watch out real good now 'cos he go bite you sometime, maybe."

"Thanks for the advice, but don't just stand there—bloody well do something, and fast!"

Moses, the old chef who ruled the roost over the other camp helpers, jumped into action and set about kicking the backsides of his underlings. As the perspicacious reader will deduce, none of this activity had the slightest effect whatsoever in persuading the snake to evacuate the tent. My PH had now arrived and, being concerned for the welfare of his client, stood well outside, asking how I was.

"Oh, I'm fine thank you," I responded. "Just nearly got blinded and then bitten to death by a spitting cobra the length and thickness of a bloody great hose pipe, that's all. You see, really nothing at all to worry about, quite trivial, except, that is, *that the thing's still in here with me*!"

"Now, now, there's no need to swear," he replied. "Your PH will save you. Keep still and try not to lose sight of the snake."

"I am keeping still, and if you don't do something soon I will be dead still!" I answered, trying to keep calm.

I heard a commotion outside and, peeping through the window flap, saw that my PH was approaching with his shotgun, which, I learned later, he had loaded with birdshot.

"Now, where is the snake?" he asked, still not putting his head into the tent.

That was the big question, because during our conversation my ghastly guest had slithered away somewhere. It was now the wild card in the pack, ready to turn up at any place and trump anybody within striking distance.

"Er, I hate to say this," I spat out with alarm, "but the blighter's cleared off somewhere. I haven't a clue where it could be."

Now, if there is anything worse than a venomous snake near to you, then it's a venomous snake near you that you can't see. I got up onto the bed and looked around the tent. No snake anywhere. I weighed up my chances and leaped from the bed and out of the tent with alacrity.

The camp personnel were assembled in a group just outside the tent door but scattered in every direction, squawking like a flock of frightened chickens before a swooping hawk, at my sudden busting forth. They ran away despite the entreaties of my PH and Moses to come back. Moses watched them for a moment and then spat emphatically in their direction and muttered something that I gathered was not too complimentary.

"Now, my friend," I said calmly, looking nonchalantly at my nails. "Be a good PH for once, will you, and just pop inside the tent and earn your daily fee and kill that big trophy snake. I'm sure it'll make the record book with plenty to spare. The bugger must be three metres long, at least."

"Now, don't swear and don't get upset over a snake; after all, you haven't been bitten have you? I will sort it out," he said in a not very convincing tone.

The others had trickled back now and were eager spectators again. After all, it wasn't every day that they had the chance to see a spitting cobra being shot to death by their Bossman. My PH, wearing a pair of shades over his eyes for protection, checked the shotgun and then pushed the flap of the tent to one side. He pointed the shotgun and fired a blast of birdshot at the snake. It was poking its head out from under the bed, he said later. He went into the tent and emerged holding the shattered serpent by the tail. The snake was twisting violently around its own body, but its head had been totally pulverized by the load of shot at very close range. My PH sounded very serious as he spoke to me, holding the snake up for all to see.

"Let that be a lesson to you. If you'd have gone hunting earlier, like a real hunter, and had not lain in bed like a sluggard, then, who knows, this very fine snake might not have been there to wake you up. And what's more, you were never in any great danger, because the snake had emptied its poison sacs spitting at you. In any case, I always have some antivenin with me in case my clients get bitten. So you see, it wasn't so bad after all. Now give us all a big smile and enjoy the rest of your hunt!"

I did, with the following exception.

The black wildebeest can be hunted in many areas of RSA these days, a result of the careful management of the stock. I hunted this animal in the Dullstroom area, which I call the Siberia of RSA.

This old bull giraffe was about twenty years old. His hide was very dark, his teeth well worn, and he was covered with ticks. RSA.

Giraffes are some of the most beautiful animals in Africa, especially old dark-skinned males. RSA. (Safari Press photo library)

Bushpigs are very difficult to hunt, being mostly nocturnal. In some places, in winter, you may catch them loitering about and get lucky. I got this magnificent trophy boar on the Nylstroom concession. RSA.

A lion from the bushveld, not Hollywood. He is in good condition and in the prime of life. Hoedspruit area, Mpumalanga, RSA.

A nice warthog male from the Transvaal. RSA. (Safari Press photo library)

Here a male warthog shows you its four warts and scalpels. Do not underestimate the courage of these feisty members of the pig family. As with all other animals, it's the dead ones that can get up and kill you. RSA.

Warthogs often kneel to get at tasty morsels. (Safari Press photo library)

Giraffes are gregarious animals, and groups like this are common. They live off the leaves other animals can't reach, but when they drink, they must spread their legs to reach the water and are then vulnerable. RSA.

The southern mountain reedbuck is a master climber, almost as good as the klipspringer. This one made the book with something to spare. RSA.

This ruggedly handsome waterbuck fell to a single shot from my .375 H&H Magnum. Waterbuck meat is not very good, but the lions we baited with this bull devoured it. Proof again that lions will eat anything! RSA.

Vervet monkeys can, unfortunately, become quite tame. This one shows his girlfriend how to beg for food from passing cars. Never feed wild animals; it is a misplaced kindness to do so, and it is only a matter of time before someone gets bitten! Kruger Park, RSA.

This mature blesbok ram scored high by Rowland Ward's criteria. Note the shoulder-shot placement: It was a bit high, but more than good enough to kill instantly with the Silvertip bullet in calibre .375 H&H Magnum. RSA.

It's not easy to get a nice, clean Burchell zebra with its ears intact and neck unscarred. I failed, but my wife showed me how! This was her first African animal and she handled it well, making a perfect shoulder shot at eighty metres. RSA.

The mountain zebra is a good climber and is usually found high up in difficult terrain. If you are successful, don't make the mistake of feeding any of the meat to dogs unless you own a gas mask! Namibia.

The striped pattern of the zebra is like a fingerprint; no two are the same. This juvenile was so busy cropping grass that he didn't notice me creeping up. Lucky for him I was not a lion! RSA.

The eland is a large antelope. The light, sandy brown hide melts into the dead grass of the bushveld. Unfortunately, this one was a cow. It was my first and, I hope, my last mistake. Saying sorry doesn't help. RSA.

Ostriches can get too friendly. Here a flock of the big birds congregate in the housing compound of the Vaalwater property. Ostriches can run faster than seventy kilometres per hour and kick and peck you to a pulp. RSA.

The diminutive steenbok is a challenge to hunt. These will o' the wisps zip into the undergrowth and have vanished long before you can even raise your rifle. I had shot this steenbok the night before this photo was taken, during the last seconds of daylight. Namibia.

This Jack Russell terrier was stitched up after having been slit open by a warthog. A year later a pack of hyenas killed him. RSA.

Black-backed jackals are among the harder to get smaller animals in southern Africa. (Safari Press photo library)

The strangely mottled brown-and-purple topi can do up to seventy kilometres per hour with a lion snapping at its tail. This old bull had been a loner for some time and in danger of being caught by lions before he could be processed into a trophy fee. RSA.

These few birds in the hand are definitely worth more than those thousands still out there in the bush. Sand grouse make challenging shooting and excellent eating. Namibia.

The ridge of white back hair on the common springbok stands on end in death and a scent of freshly baked bread pervades the air. This spectacle is soon over, and the patch of white hair will collapse. Namibia.

A small group of sable antelope. The grass is dry, but that's probably what sable like to eat—dry grass! RSA.

When hunting, you sometimes have to get above the bush in order to see anything. We found this wind-driven water pump out in the bush and climbed up. Note the big bird's nest above us. Mpumalanga, RSA.

The helmeted guinea fowl is everywhere in the bush. It is a challenging game bird to shoot, and the meat is excellent. Lead them well and use heavy loads in your shotgun. And don't forget your umbrella—they are expert bombers! RSA.

Hunting in Africa means more than big game. Try shooting birds for a change. Here you see the results of some lucky shots and the resulting sand grouse. This is a much more gentlemanly bird than the guinea! Namibia.

Common eland are found in South Africa, Botswana, Namibia, and Zimbabwe. This female was photographed in Zimbabwe. (Safari Press photo library)

This is a very old and partially blind eland cow. The game farmer has kept her in a spacious, lion-safe compound for the last ten years; eland can become quite tame in captivity. Mpumalanga, RSA.

Chapter 11

Snake Trilogy: Twig Snake

There was something wrong with the season because we'd seen plenty of them already. They lay on sandbars, slithered off the road, or hung coiled around branches. They were green, brown, blackish nondescript, and white blotched, and varied in size from pencil-thin to a man's thigh thick. They watched you carefully and coldly. Some even hissed at you if you came too close. This latter experience plays havoc with your nerves, and everyone tends to get jumpy. Some were short-tempered and challenging; others, more wary, slipped away silently into the cover. Some were poisonous; others were not. They all frightened the hell out of you, though. They had shed their skins everywhere. The pale sheaths of scales were draped over rocks, left on the bush tracks, or impaled on twigs, left to flutter in the breeze. No matter what colour, size, or texture the skins were, they had a common denominator: They all originated from snakes.

We had already seen several puff adders (*Bitis arietans*) in the Vaalwater concession, South Africa. These snakes of the viper family have a bite that will inject you with agonizing venom that will either send you to Valhalla or cause massive sloughing of your flesh and skin and a ghastly secondary infection. You can lose a limb from this. The vipers have a hematoxic venom that affects the blood and tissues. Bites from these snakes are very painful. Invariably, they lie lethargically like plump brown and white harlequin-patterned slugs, seemingly just waiting for anything to tread on them. We didn't oblige. We had even watched a thick python sliding down a hole in the ground. Summing up, the snakes were everywhere you looked and it was, therefore, definitely not a good place or time to hunt. It is nerve-racking to try to stalk, watching in front for the game and keeping an eye on the ground, at the same time, for such things as slithering black mambas, cobras, and puff adders. An eye should also be kept open for the emerald green mambas and twig snakes up in the bushes and trees. Too bad, we didn't have enough eyes to go around.

Trouble with Twig Snakes

We were stalking a warthog for rations. The animal had seen us and taken alarm, for it had guessed our murderous intentions to turn him into pork pie. It set off at a brisk trot, and had gone down a riverbank and disappeared into the bushes. We waited, and then Peacock, our tracker, took the spoor up again, easily reading the sign. The sun basted us with its heat, and sweat trickled like transparent snakes into our eyes and stung them bloodshot. We went farther down the riverbank, which now narrowed as the river squeezed itself down some rapids and into a high-walled valley. The warthog had passed this way and we followed, Peacock leading the way. The bush was getting so dense now that we had to continually push the greenery away from our faces.

Suddenly, with a shriek of "*noga!*" (snake!) Peacock jumped backward.

The twig snake is a master of camouflage, and it is therefore easy to come into contact with this particular piece of bad news. The snake is rear-fanged, or opisthoglyph; its fangs are grooved, allowing the venom to enter the prey during swallowing. A dose of twig snake venom will require that you have a total blood transfusion, because there is no antidote. The venom contains an enzyme that stops blood from coagulating. This means that you will bleed to death if you don't get a bloodchange. In less than half an hour you will start bleeding from the bitten place, your gums, and even yesterday's razor nick. Your nose will bleed as if someone has just punched it for you, and you may vomit black blood if you happen to have a stomach ulcer. Don't bother looking for the milk of magnesia. This noncoagulation can persist for weeks. That makes it a singularly unpleasant business, and I could think of much better things to do than to lie in hospital and get bled-out to get bled-in. Fortunately, the twig snake is not very aggressive. When disturbed it will try to escape rather than share its venom with you, which is jolly decent of it. Since the snake's venom fangs are situated well back, it has to get hold of your finger or the edge of your hand to cause you trouble. Don't try a karate chop on this one!

The snake lay along the branches of the bush. Occasionally it flicked its tongue at us to pick up our scent. We had recovered from the surprise and now stood admiring the perfect camouflage of the snake. The blend of colours was subtle, and it was evident that any small bird or lizard would have a hard job to spot the dappled danger lying there. We skirted the bush, and the snake remained where it was.

Picking up the warthog's spoor, we carried on. But not for long. Again Peacock jumped back. Two twig snakes were slowly coiling themselves around each other. These close encounters were not doing wonders for our nerves. I'd had enough excitement for the day.

I looked at my PH.

"I think we have blundered into a twig snake love-in or something. The damn things are everywhere. I vote that we leave them to their business and forget that warthog."

"I agree," he said, in obvious relief. "These snakes make stalking hell on earth. Let's get back before we get unlucky and one of them decides to see what we taste like."

We about-turned and gingerly picked our way back through the bushes. We encountered three more "twiggies"; it was a weird feeling to know that we had passed this way not long before and that the snakes had almost certainly been nearby. I quickened my pace. Back at the Jeep we cured our thirst, calmed our nerves, and drove off, leaving the place to the snakes.

Chapter 12

Dangerous Things and an Underrated Bird

There is no answer to the question "Which is the most dangerous animal in South Africa?" It will depend on one's experience. If you've been held up and robbed in a big city there, you might be justified in saying that people are quite dangerous. Others, who have been butted by buffalo or scared by snakes, will also have something to say as to which they think is the most dangerous. The list of dangerous things in Africa just about covers everything that flies, creeps, swims, slithers, crawls, runs, or walks. And that's leaving out biting insects and poisonous plants.

I believe that the most dangerous creatures are those that have had human contact and have then been released to the wild. They have no inherent fear of humans and appear tame. People from the cities are thrilled to bits when a "tame" member of the bush family comes up to their car. For instance, Granny would just love to have a photo of herself holding hands with that nice old friendly baboon

("Oh, what large teeth you have, granny!"). That lion over there looks as though he wouldn't hurt a fly, and little Johnny wants a photo too. And so on. Don't take my word for it; read any newspaper from Africa and you will see how deadly stupid people can be. I'll now tell you an experience I had with a "tame" bird.

In my estimation, ostriches (*Struthio camelus*) are underrated as dangerous creatures. These largest of birds, weighing one hundred and fifty kilograms, cannot fly; they don't need to, since they can run at seventy kilometres per hour and kick like turbo-assisted mules. The cock is irritable when sitting on the eggs that its various hens have deposited in a scratched-out depression in the sand that does for a nest. The eggs weigh one and a half kilograms and hatch about forty-two days after being laid. The big birds can live up to seventy years; I'll bet *that's* tough meat.

Ostriches can deal you a hefty peck. If your eye or nose connects with an ostrich, the least of your worries is a lost eye; the plastic surgery to restore your profile could work out to be more expensive. Not only is the power of the kick devastating, but the large, main toenail is capable of splitting you open enough for you to take a look at your insides before you pass out, and pass on. Lions have been found disemboweled after an encounter with an ostrich with a bad hangover. Even I had a close brush with a tame ostrich some years ago. Let me tell you about it.

I was hunting blesbok (*Damaliscus dorcas phillipsi*), a beautifully marked reddish brown antelope with a white patch on the front of its face and brown-black ivory-ringed horns that turn inside. This antelope, like its near cousin the bontebok (*Damaliscus dorcas dorcas*), was nearly eradicated by excessive farming and hunting, but, thanks to game management, viable herds now exist. The blesbok was in thick thornbush, and we had to make the stalk under variable wind conditions. That was a problem, but a far greater one was the ostrich. You see, a tame cock ostrich that some congenital idiot had raised from a chick had decided that we needed his company and took to following us at a very indiscreet distance. The bloody bird had already spoiled a shot at the blesbok by wandering between the quarry and me at the critical moment. The blesbok had quickly weighed up the situation and had made off into the thicket. We took to throwing clods of earth at the barmy bird, who just regarded the missiles as offerings and inspected each one carefully to see if it contained anything edible. It seemed that it was waiting for things to be thrown at it, and I must say, it was expert in avoiding direct hits. In retrospect, I reckon it must have had a lot of practice. Everywhere we went he followed us like a feathered dog.

We had stopped for a while to allow the blesbok to settle down and to take refreshment. My PH's wife had packed us a few sandwiches, and the beer came out of the box nicely frosted. We regarded our snacks and drinks with relish, but so did the ostrich. It had now come near and was avidly inspecting our picnic. It was quite impressed with it all. Its big eyes, surrounded by ridiculous fluttering eyelashes long enough to make any Hollywood actress green with envy, swept over our provisions. Then, with one snap of its beak, it stabbed forward and plucked my lettuce sandwich out of my hand. The movement was so practiced, quick, and precise that my lunch had already vanished down its white, elastic throat (you could clearly see the descent of the sandwich) before I could drop my hand. Just imagine the damage inflicted if the bird had fancied a peck at me instead of my lunch. (OK, I might have ended up more handsome than I am at present, but that's beside the point.)

To say that I was shaken is an understatement, and when I had recovered, I seriously contemplated settling the bird's account with buckshot. But then, it had not done me any direct harm and was clearly interested only in food and company. It was oblivious to the fact that we didn't need its company. This is always the problem when people take a baby creature out of the wild and proceed to make it "tame." A baby lion or leopard sure is cute, but the kittens grow up to be very big cats. Meat-eating predators, in fact. Predators that have lost their natural fear of man. This makes them both dangerous and candidates for being shot when they bite or kill a human. Clearly, this serves no one, least of all the animals in question. The handfeeding of wild animals makes them dependent on humans, and the animals gradually lose their ability to look after themselves.

P.S. We got the blesbok later on in the day, despite the unwanted company.

Chapter 13

Ticks and Fever

The place was near the northeastern border with Swaziland, in southern Africa, and I was there to shoot a problem hippo that had taken to chasing natives and devouring their crops. The *kubu* was a bull, and he was playing havoc as only hippos can. The people were frightened to go out to tend the pathetic remains of their horticultural efforts, even during the day. The hippo was a crafty old beggar as well, since he would disappear into the neighbouring nature reserve, where all hunting was forbidden, after he had filled his immense paunch. We had arrived at the area in the late afternoon, since my PH's Jeep had chosen to break down and leave its guts, in the form of the entire exhaust system, on the road between Barberton and Bulembu. We had just enough time to zero in the rifle with full-jacket bullets before darkness fell.

Away from the hunting area, we were quartered in spacious canvas tents that had every luxury and convenience imaginable. After a wash and a change of clothes, we had a late dinner. Over coffee and cognac, we discussed the coming hunt. We decided that we would walk along the riverbank, as early as shooting light would allow, and see if we could take care of business and be off for the rest of the hunt within a day. Theory and practice are different, though.

I got back to my tent and felt the fatigue of the day and the cognac take effect. When I had closed the mosquito net around me, I fell safely into the arms of Morpheus. Well, "safely" is only a relative word, since I was safe only from large animals. It was the small ones that got me. That night I was devoured.

We had noticed that the ticks (*Ixodidae species*) were very bad that year. Although the *bos luis* (bush lice) are bad enough any year, this time they were worse. They infested the whole place, just lying, waiting for you to get near. And when they found you, they would crawl, unnoticed, over clothes and seek out the places into which they could bore their proboscises. They would then suck your blood, like milk through a straw. In this endeavour they were depressingly successful, and, at the end of the day, after creeping after some trophy or another, you had to strip off and hunt the animals on your body. The bush and pepper ticks were to be found invariably in the most delicate of locations. Armpits and, worst of all, scrotums, were not free from their visits, and a damn nuisance they were, too. You see, the places where they had fed itched like mad afterward, and it is not very good social etiquette, even in the bush, to be seen scratching at your genitals like a monkey.

The other problem with ticks, which are related to spiders, since they have eight legs, is that they can carry a variety of illnesses that they impart to you during the act of bloodsucking. They are proven vectors for some unpleasant illnesses, such as tick fever, Lyme disease, and meningitis. Also, ticks belong to the category of poisonous creatures like scorpions, spiders, and wasps, since some varieties can fill you in addition with nasty toxins that cause weakness and paralysis of the muscles. Other symptoms following a nip from a tick include loss of feeling in the affected part, a prickling in the mouth and lips, splitting headache, loss of appetite, and the urge to vomit.

Not finishing here, very great care must be exercised when removing a tick. Once it has bitten into you, the head is firmly anchored to the harpoon-barbed proboscis, and if the body is ripped away the head is likely to remain in your skin to cause a secondary pustule of infection. Ticks are a nuisance to everything and anything that walks or flies in the bush, except, I imagine, themselves. All game suffers from their visits, and some animals such as warthogs, rhinos, and elephants go into mud wallows to try to suffocate the parasites. The possibility of contracting a tick-borne disease during a hunt is quite high. Tick fever can knock you out and leave you weak as a kitten for up to a month. This is not good, if you had intended to hunt.

Morning came, and now, whilst I was washing and shaving, I became aware of an itch under my right armpit. I inspected the region and saw that legions of pepper ticks had started a banquet there. The ticks must have been in the grass where we had sighted in the rifle the night before. The parasites had all bitten in solidly. My first attempt to remove one ended up with its head left embedded in my skin and its body, complete with dismally waving legs, in the tweezers. Not a success. I noticed that my whole arm was a pale red colour, caused by the anticoagulant the pests had already spit into me. The only way to remove the ticks was to twist them out carefully. After a while I had got them all out, although my arm was, by then, as red as a cooked lobster.

The de-ticking session had spoiled our plans to make an early start. We therefore set off with the sun already high in the sky in the hope that the hippo would still be around. It wasn't. It wasn't the day after, either. On the third day we heard that the *kubu* had taken up residence at the other end of the nature reserve and, as such, was no longer an official nuisance animal.

Not wanting to lose any more time, we left the region to continue with the hunt. Three days later I fell ill with tick fever. Lying in my fever-tossed bed and sweat-sodden sheets, with a headache worse than a cognac hangover could ever manage, I declared war on ticks. Those sons-of-bitches, not content with robbing my blood, had also given me a raging fever. And my hunting days were going. I sweated it out in my tent for two days before I again felt strong enough to hold my rifle. Toward the end of the safari, we heard that the bull hippo had returned to his old place and had brought reinforcements in the shape of a wife. I wished them a good appetite. There was no way that I was ever going back to that place.

Chapter 14

Mosquitoes, Malaria, and Other Torments

Mosquitoes (*Anopheles* species), as you probably know, are a vector for the malaria parasite. That's a fact of life. And death. The exact number of humans that become infected with malaria in Africa each year is not known, but it's a few million at least. The earlier worldwide mosquito eradication schemes failed, and the DDT insecticide assault made only a slight dent in the armour of the insects. Subsequent banning of DDT, for environmental considerations, has been welcomed by all, especially the malaria-carrying mosquito.

We have other plans than to lie groaning in sweat-soaked blankets, fever-racked and shivering, don't we? So swallow your malaria prophylactic tablet, hope that a nonresistant strain of malaria is waiting for you, smear on some insect repellent, hope that it works, and come into a malaria area with me. Don't worry; everything will be all right. Well, maybe.

The area of South Africa called Mpumalanga is classified as a malarial region, and one should take preventative medicine before visiting there. The worst time for malaria is in the summer, when there is plenty of water and warmth, both essential for the breeding and well-being of mosquitoes. Fortunately, most hunting takes place in winter, when the dry, cold conditions are unfavourable for "mossies."

The mosquito injects saliva into you with its needle-sharp proboscis before drinking your blood. The saliva contains an anticoagulant, but also a phase of the malaria parasite cycle. One way to combat malaria is to take preventative medicine. I had heard from my PH that he had some new antimalaria prophylax and that it was much less expensive than the medicine I got from back home. This potent pill had to be taken only once a week during the hunt and again a week after leaving the malarial region. He handed me the medicine upon my arrival for my next hunt.

"Everybody takes these," he said. "They are mighty powerful stuff, and you will be safe from malaria, at a much lower cost." He placed the bill from the apothecary into my hand. "Take the first one now and let's be off into the bush hunting, instead of worrying about mosquitoes and malaria!"

I popped the tiny pink tablet out of its aluminum-foil cocoon and swilled the bitter-tasting chip of chemical hope down my throat with water. I was ready to hunt.

It was early March and still summertime, meaning that mosquitoes were still active. Despite this, we were hunting leopard. We were near an oily brown lake, and the bushes bordering it seethed and roiled with biting insects that came out in droves when we took our place in the blind. As we waited for the leopard, which never did come, the insects dive-bombed us with high-pitched engines screaming at full revs. Between the incessant piping of the frogs and the whining dive of the kamikaze insect dive bombers it was a noisy, unpleasant place; no wonder the *ingwe* never came. If sound could be coloured, that place would have been a three-dimensional kaleidoscope.

The blasted bloodsuckers had an uncanny knack for finding the tiniest piece of exposed skin and would instantly bore their diamond-tipped hypodermic-needle noses into you. They would relieve you of a litre or two of blood and leave you with an itch that lasted forever. There was another sort of winged nuisance that didn't even bother to find bare skin; it just stuck into you, right through your clothes and through the barrier of repellent. I think the repellent was addictive to them, and they came in droves to imbibe the stuff, like an aperitif before the main course of blood. I was so badly bitten one night that my face became a single red pimple. That was all right, though, despite its being uncomfortable, because I knew that I wouldn't get malaria, thanks to the tablets.

As time went on, I got concerned about the power of the tablets and decided to take another one, just to make sure, making my consumption two tablets in a week. Each night we went to wait for the leopard, and each night we became a full-course meal for the insect equivalent of Count Dracula. I reckoned that I lost about three litres of blood at each sitting, but my PH reckoned it wasn't so bad—only about half that much. At the end of the first week I had taken three of the tablets; I was making certain that I wouldn't get malaria. By the end of the second week I'd taken another four.

One morning, at the start of the last week, I awoke to an intense itching all over my body. I stumbled out of bed, thinking that I'd slept in a nest of fleas. It was still dark, but I could feel that my body was covered with thick, raised welts, as if someone had been flaying me with a hippo-hide whip. The itch was unbearable, so I went into the shower and stood shivering as the icy needles of water pounded relief at me. It took some heat out the itchiness.

After about five minutes, I felt sufficiently numb to inspect the damage. The damage assessment was not good. My body was covered in large red patches that rose like islands on a white sea. As the shower-induced anesthetic wore off, the itching came back. I was going crazy with the tickling, and I suppose I realized then where the saying "tickled to death" must come from. There is no more disagreeable sensation one can encounter than an itch, excepting your tax payment demand, that is. A bad itch is conducive to insanity. I felt like thrashing around on the floor (just as I do when I receive my tax bill), to get at the itchy patches on my back. I returned to the shower instead. I was still alternating between sanity and insanity (in the shower and out again) when my PH came over to find out where I was and if I wanted any breakfast before going hunting. He took a look at my scarlet skin.

"Are you a new client? I thought I had a white man here. Now, what have you been doing? Did you stand too much in the sun?"

I was in no mood for jokes.

"Look here, while you were asleep, your client was being eaten alive by God knows what," I rejoined. "I reckon you've got an invasion from fleas, or something more sinister."

"That can't be! We always clean everything out daily and spray the floorboards against creeping things. Anyway, that skin eruption does not look like a bite," he said, taking a step backward. "Maybe you are coming down with some unknown tropical illness," he added, taking another step toward the door.

I had to agree with him. Normally when one is bitten or stung, there is a puncture mark in the middle of the inflamed region.

"Maybe it's an allergy. But I can't think of anything we've eaten that was out of the ordinary," I said, morosely scratching at a bright red patch of skin.

"Well, you'd better put something on. That wet towel will give you a cold. We'll go to the doctor when you are ready," he said, disappearing quickly from my room.

The drive to the doctor was itching hell on earth. Even the thin silk shirt I wore tickled my skin like a feather. The doctor examined me, slowly nodding his head.

"Yes, I've seen all this before. Tell me, have you been taking the new antimalaria pills?"

He nodded his head more rapidly to my affirmative answer.

"You've taken too many, and now you've an allergic reaction. You should keep strictly to the dosage suggested. If you exceed the dose, you get this allergy trouble. The only thing to do is to stop taking the pills and not to scratch. I'll give you some lotion to lessen the itch."

"Yes, I admit I've taken a few, but I was worried about malaria," I replied.

"There is no need. These pills are very effective. As you are going back home soon, you needn't take any more. You've enough medicine in your bloodstream to kill anything."

"Yes, I told him that they were mighty powerful stuff," rejoined my PH, eyes gleaming with suppressed mirth.

I reflected that you can't win in Africa. Try to prevent illness and you get an allergy. Do nothing and join the malaria club. I never did take any more of that medicine, nor have I had malaria, either.

Chapter 15

Of Honey Badgers and Men

We were hunting on a concession of some seven thousand hectares of unspoilt land near to Vaalwater, about three hours' drive due north of Johannesburg, South Africa. We were told by the owner that there was some poaching going on and had been asked to keep a lookout. Our hunt this morning had produced a few helmeted guinea fowl that we had brought down in flight using 12-gauge magnum shotguns. Driving along a dry riverbed, we noticed a pair of jackals circling a bush. The black-backed jackals (*Canis mesomelas*) are mostly nocturnal animals that fill the ecological function of garbage cleaners. In this the animal is very efficient, and usually there is nothing left of any dead animal after twenty-four hours in the bush. What the jackals miss, the vultures and hyenas finish off. And vice versa.

It is unusual to see jackals in the daytime, and the way they were going on aroused our interest. We drove past the jackals and were surprised that these timid animals moved only a small distance away; there was something suspicious here. Buckshot shells were slid into shotguns and we went to investigate. We got to within fifteen metres of the bush and all hell broke loose. The honey badger exploded from out of the bushes and came for us with the determination of a Spanish fighting bull of the Midra breed. It came to an abrupt halt as the sling around its front paw reached its maximum length. The honey badger made a chattering screech like dry disc brakes. It stood, swaying from side to side in pent-up anger, watching us. Its black, beady eyes took in every movement we made. Each movement provoked the chattering. We had a fair idea what the devil would do to us, if it were free. Its yellowish white fangs were bared in a rictus of malevolence, and we instinctively moved back a few steps. It screeched at us again. It was truly awesome to see the impressive biting equipment that the animal possessed.

Everything in Africa respects the honey badger (*Mellivora capensis*); its resilience, courage, and sheer tenacity in attack or defense are legendary. Honey badgers are somewhat smaller than the European badger (*Meles meles*) and have a silvery pale skullcap of fur that merges into a silver gray overcoat. They wear black belly fur that goes on to the paws, which are fitted out with long black claws that are permanently extended. The animals are impervious to the stings of termites, ants, and bees when ripping open their nests for grubs and honey. They have an interesting relationship with the honey guide bird (*Indicator indicator*). The bird will lead the badger to a wild bee's nest and let it do the work of breaking it open. The badger gets honey and grubs, and the bird gets grubs and the wax, which it is specially adapted to digest. Even hyenas and lions prefer to move out of the way of a foraging honey badger. This honey badger had obviously blundered into a poacher's snare during the night. The jackals, opportunists par excellence, had come across it and were not ready to give up the chance of an easy meal, hence their reluctance to leave.

Honey badgers are protected in South Africa, so we decided to free this specimen from its predicament if possible. Having taken this decision, the next problem to be solved was how to release the badger. After much discussion with our black helper, Peacock, we decided to bind two stout branches together at one end and thus make a sort of wooden pitchfork. The open end would be used to pin the head of the beast. This would allow some brave person, yet to be chosen, to apply a pair of cutting pliers to the wire of the sling and then put a dose of iodine onto the paw, where the wire had cut to the bone.

It was a nice theoretical solution to a practical problem, if ever there was one. A suitable "pitchfork" was soon made. We stood watching the badger. It had now calmed down a little. It had ceased to screech at us and was content now to bare its teeth in a manner designed to let you know what it would do to you if it were free.

I started to open my case, carefully, like a defense lawyer, detailing why my PH should have the honour of performing the rescue and thereby do his good deed for the day. "Look," I said, in what I thought to be a very reasonable and convincing tone. "That badger won't do anything. It will be grateful when it is freed. Don't you remember the story of Androcles and the lion? Androcles really had a way with cats, and they could sense it. They loved him, I swear it. When one had a thorn in its paw, it came straight to him and our pal Androcles wasn't scared. He just did his duty and removed that terrible thorn.

"Later on, when he was in big trouble in the arena and the lions were let loose to eat him, his good friend—you know, the lion with the thorn—recognized him. It only licked him. Imagine that! I'm telling you straight; the Romans loved it and gave Androcles a pardon, and they all lived happily ever after. Just imagine, you and a honey badger starting a lifelong friendship. At the least, you can be content about having saved a member of a protected species. It's even settled down now and is quite used to us. In fact, I think that it is smiling at us and not baring its teeth, as might be misconstrued. Actually, it has beautiful teeth, and I get the feeling, already, that it quite likes you. It knows you don't mean it any harm."

"Yeah," replied my PH uncertainly. "But I'm telling you straight that we have a honey badger here and not a mere lion. That badger is capable of ripping a bigger piece of rump steak out of your ass, and quicker, than a lion ever could if things go wrong."

I could tell that his resolve was weakening, so, looking carefully at my nails, I pressed home my attack.

"Ah! Don't you see?" I cajoled. "That's the whole point. Nothing can go wrong, and think of all the credit you'll get. Anyway, I don't see why I should do it, because, after all, I'm the client and I am paying you lots of bucks to conduct me and protect me from all sorts of things in the bush."

"I couldn't care less about that!" he retorted. "I'm telling you straight, and finally, there's absolutely no way that you'll even get me near to that bloody thing. Just look at the size of that nasty little bugger's teeth. They're big enough to make a shark jealous!"

Five minutes later, our PH stood before us. His face was pallid, but, if you ignored that, he looked resplendent with the iodine bottle in one hand and a pair of pliers in the other. Peacock, in his raggedy pants and T-shirt, stood like an incongruous knight at a jousting tournament, carrying the big wooden pinchers like a lance. I had retreated into a tree at what seemed to me a safe distance, having care not to get too far away to miss the action or to be called a coward. Peacock and my PH now approached the snared badger. It watched them with increasing interest and had stopped its teeth castanets from clicking. It now cocked its head a bit to the side, the portent of things to come. In one deft movement, Peacock got the unfortunate animal's head pinned down. The ire of the badger was at full pitch, as evidenced by the ear-piercing, shrill-as-a-siren shriek it let out. I got the distinct impression that it was cussing in badger language. I was right. Anyway, my PH applied the pliers and then, freeing the ends of the filthy, blood-sodden wire, unscrewed the iodine bottle and prepared to disinfect the wound.

Now, the desirable effect of iodine on an open wound is to cause disinfection. Unfortunately, it has an undesirable side effect—namely, that once applied to a wound it burns hotter than napalm. We were about to find out that even honey badgers are not immune to this. None of us were prepared for what followed the application of the healing tincture. The badger first lay still, then, wriggling like a barrel full of eels, the pain-crazed beast lifted its head out of the undignified position it was in. It twisted with the strength of a maniac, bit straight through one of the tines of the pitchfork, and made for the nearest victim it could reach. Peacock, always well aware of danger, had already beaten the Olympic record for the fifty-metre dash and was up the same tree as yours truly, watching the interesting scene developing below.

This left our PH to face the music. The honey badger, beside itself with rage, teeth chattering like a road drill, squared up and sprang at its tormentor and got its teeth embedded in my PH's left boot. He fell over, and the badger was so surprised that it let go, momentarily. Never one to look a gift horse in the mouth, my PH sprang to his feet and was off in a flash. The badger took off after him, screeching like a demented banshee. It was a close one before our reluctant Olympic sprinter could vault into the welcoming branches of a nearby thorn tree and escape the snapping teeth a fraction behind his behind. Well, "welcoming" is only a relative term because, judging from the curses emanating from somewhere in the top of the prickly throne, he was getting a lot of thorn up there. The badger milled around the base of the tree, looking for a way up, but saw the idiocy of going up there and ran off. We slowly got down, feeling a little sheepish, and then Peacock started to laugh. The emotion was infectious, and soon we were all hooting with laughter like hyenas. We recovered, and, still clutching our aching sides, climbed, weak-kneed with mirth, into the Jeep.

On the way home, my PH complained and bit thorns out of the back of his hand. I noticed, too, that he was sitting in a peculiar position, and every now and then, especially when the Jeep bucked over a pothole, I saw him wince. He was evasive about my question as to his well-being, but he knew that I was on to him, all right! I requested that he stop the Jeep, which he did with a sigh of resignation. I asked him to get out of the Jeep, which he did, slowly. I ordered him to drop his trousers. He did, slowly and very reluctantly, and Peacock and I searched the vast pimply white buttocks now bared before us. Not a pleasant job or a nice sight, either, I can assure you. I had already delved into the first-aid box and I soon saw what I was after. I applied the tweezers to the black hole in his right buttock and removed the thorn that had been embedded there. I triumphantly showed him the cause of his discomfort, waving it before his face like a hunting trophy. Then I doused the whole area with iodine. It was like putting a match to a firework: Light the blue touch paper and retire. It took about two seconds before the stuff bit into the open wound. He writhed as he came to terms with the terrible tincture. I became philosophical.

"Now, now, it's nothing. Look at it this way. You rescue a badger and then you maltreat it by nearly burning its paw off with iodine. It tried to settle the score, but you ran away like the abject coward that you are and hid in a tree. You got an inch-long thorn in your fat ass for your troubles. Your kind friends helped you to get rid of the thorn and, ever watchful for the health and safety of the PH, disinfected it with the same tincture that you had applied to the badger. You have learnt that both professional hunters and honey badgers are sensitive to the action of iodine tincture on raw wounds. In addition, you have seen how fast a honey badger can run. Objectively, it's been quite an informative day for us all. I think that from this day onward we should call you Androcles." I hadn't better record his reply. Censorship, you know.

Chapter 16

Rogues

The following has nothing to do with what you thought it did. Sorry to disappoint you if you were expecting tales of mass destruction caused by pain-crazed elephants, buffaloes, and suchlike. Rogues, as in scoundrels, are all over the place. As with everything in this money-driven world, hunting is also subject to market forces. Recognizing this, some enterprising people (that is, the rogues) have seized the chance to make money with the invention of the instant, safe, guaranteed, no-nonsense hunting trophy "out of a can." The principle of supply and demand is the driving force behind this unsavoury and unethical practice. Imagine the following.

Fifty-seven Varieties

The senile circus lion is brought out from its cage and its tearful trainer kisses it good-bye. Yes, kisses it because he's hand raised the pussycat from a cub that was born in captivity. He's worked with it for years, and they have a relationship more like that of a man and his dog. The arthritic cat hobbles out into the transport wagon and is pushed into a cage. The doors are slammed closed, and it is brought out to a large enclosure somewhere deep on a game ranch to await the arrival of an unsuspecting hunter.

The hunter has booked a lion safari and has been told there are a few lions about, including a good old one. He arrives full with the hope of a fair chase and a trophy lion. The rogue takes him out hunting but there is never a sign of the lion, since the supplier of canned lion makes sure he doesn't drive too near its enclosure. At night, watching the stars twinkle and still dreaming of his lion, the client thrills to hear the lion roar. It roars because a black helper has just popped a bit of food into its enclosure. The old cat is happy. The meat is easy to chew with his few remaining teeth.

The hunter is kept dangling for days; days for which he pays a hefty Big Five daily rate. The lion, he is assured, has been seen, and, although the hunter has now only two days left, it's certain that they will get lucky. They do. The hunter is brought to the enclosure via a devious route so that he has no idea where low barriers or game fences start or finish. Surprise, surprise, there is a lion with a mane like the one from Hollywood and, after the loud bang of the rifle and the quieter click of cameras, it is duly entered into the record book.

Such practices have occurred in the past, and they still go on. It's not only with lions, either. Rhino and Cape buffalo are also candidates for the "cannery." Leopard is a bit more difficult to "can," but anything is possible, I suppose. The above practices have absolutely nothing to do with ethical hunting, and further comment is avoided here because of my rapidly rising blood pressure.

The Bad PH

There are rogues all over the place. One of the worst I met was a PH whom I shall call "Dead-eye Dick." If ever this wart-nosed weasel reads this, he will recognize himself, instantly. This person had a macho complex and charged the earth for a less than satisfactory service. He gave me food the purgative action of which caused such a violent attack that it could have cornered the world market in laxatives. And the wine was sour, too. One night I put a cartridge in a glass and poured over it the wine he had served me. The next day, the brass case was eaten right through to the powder. Talk about rotgut! After any meal served out of the kitchen of old Dead-eye you would get heartburn hotter than an eruption from Mount Vesuvius. All this for the princely sum of $800 US per day. I was stranded with this person, so I had to get on with it.

Dead-eye Dick had a bad camp, all right. The latrines stunk so much that they hummed like an electricity transformer. The air was so thick with odour and flies that you had to hold your hand over your mouth to avoid an involuntary meal of insects and to block the stink. Swarms of blue and green flies patrolled the area, waiting to savour the next moist fecal offerings to be jettisoned into that pit of purgatory and gastric rejection by Dickie's unhappy clients. You can imagine that a pit in the ground, filled to the brim with the ejected and partially processed rubbish served in Dickie's kitchen, is a fairly good runner-up for Dante's inferno. It nearly was. Let me explain.

After a dreadful, stormy night of stomach cramp and hurricane gusts of breaking wind, I gave up my gastric struggle to retain some of Dickie's food and dragged my miserable self over to the latrines. It was early and still dark. Having no flashlight (Dickie had the only one, for himself), I walked carefully over to the dreaded pit. Easing myself onto the poles, I got into position and let it all go. As I hung there, limp as a dead fly in a spider's web, I searched my pockets and came up with a packet of cigarettes and a box of matches. I convinced myself that the smoke would combat the stink. It was as good an excuse as any, although I'd really given up the filthy habit of smoking, hadn't I? I lit one up and dropped the match behind me. The next moment, a dull popping sound emanated from underneath me and a pale blue flame reached up from below. It succeeded in slightly singeing some very personal parts. I jumped off the pit rather quickly. Flammable methane gas had accumulated through the fearful fermentation processes going on in that latrine. The burning match was all that it was waiting for to ignite. I decided then to take a canary with me, the next time, just as the coal miners used to do. I told Dickie about the explosive properties of his latrines, and he only roared with laughter. Worse still, he told all the native boys, and, as a result of their mirth-making, I became known as the bwana who farts fire!

Dickie had sent me a brochure with all sorts of animal trophy prices in it, and I, like a hungry leopard, took the bait. When I got there, no animals were available, and if they were, they were not at the prices stated. They were, of course, much more expensive. There was, for example, a problem elephant going for $6,000 US (in the brochure); he requested $18,000 US when I was there. I told him that there was no way I would entertain such a thing. I told him to keep it. I wasn't that eager to part with so much money (and I didn't have it, either!) The new price was merely three times the advertised price. And so it went. I reported it all to the right places afterward, though, of that you can be sure.

Dead-eye Dick also had the tiresome habit of firing the very instant I shot. He was the instant backup man, and I am sure that his bullets got to the animals before mine did. I became fed up with Dead-eye Dick and his ways, and we parted company, never to meet again. I went hunting the following year in South Africa, and old Dead-eye heard about it and tried to get my hunt stopped. He reckoned that my new PH had "poached" me away from him! The audacity of the man was unbelievable. I wrote several missives of particularly incisive text to the right places. I sent copies of them to Dickie. At last he understood that I didn't want his "services" anymore. I've never heard about him since. Maybe a lion ate him. I really hope so. They do say that lions will eat anything.

Chapter 17

Other Dangers of Hunting

Any human activity is associated with some degree of danger. Even if you attend knitting classes, there is some risk that someone will accidentally (or purposely) jab you to death with a long needle. Whether it is driving, walking, sailing, or fishing there are many devious but efficient ways of prematurely getting yourself a piece of marble with your name chipped into it. If you have read this far, by now I think you would agree that hunting is no exception. Particularly when the hunter gets an overdose of buffalo, lion, snake, or disease, or gets in the way of a bullet, things can get very dangerous. Old Papa Hemingway wrote of such things in "The Snows of Kilimanjaro" and "The Short Happy Life of Francis Macomber." Death is one thing, disablement another. Following are just a few disabling things to watch out for if you want to live a long and happy life.

Ears

Now, if you listen to me, I'll tell you about an unpleasant thing called tinnitus, which is an occupational hazard for hunters. Tinnitus is defined as the sensation of hearing a ringing noise without external cause. That, briefly, is it. Far more, though, the ringing can come and go in volume, sounding like Big Ben one moment and then a strident telephone the next, before switching over to a buzz like a hive of bumblebees. Wads of cotton wool, rammed with enthusiasm into earholes the way a musketeer loads his muzzleloader, do not stop the noise, either. Mind over matter also fails; it's always with you. Of course, there was an external cause. That was a big bang (or many of them) from a rifle. The sound waves are so strong that they pile onto your eardrum and overload the delicate mechanism there, leaving it permanently damaged. No operation or medicine will put it right, although the condition can be avoided if you use commercially available plastic earplugs when shooting and avoid exposure to unnecessary gunfire. If you haven't got store-bought plugs, then cotton wool plugs may well save you from hearing bells for the rest of your life. Now they tell me!

Blue Shoulder and Red Eyebrow Syndrome

Hunting, besides falling under the combined laws of chance and Murphy, is also subject to the laws of physics. Until now, I have mentioned bullets, speeds, and energies in specific cases. I have also referred to kick or recoil, that unpleasant side effect you feel when a rifle fires a bullet. Let's now examine recoil in a bit more detail, without drowning in the Stygian depths of physics.

Many years ago, a fellow called Isaac Newton was nearly brained by an apple (who says fruit is good for you?) and worked out a few relationships to do with motion and gravity. The laws he formulated then still hold good today.

One of the most important for hunters is this one: "For every action there is an equal and opposite reaction." In practical terms for the hunter, this means that the faster and heavier the bullet, the more the rifle-butt kick on your shoulder. The lighter your rifle for a given bullet load, the more recoil you will feel. Recoil is a weird thing. If you are shooting at paper targets, checking your telescope's setting, you feel every punishing thump of the rifle as your shoulder is slowly churned into a black and purple patch. Stalk an animal and shoot it, and you don't feel a thing. Mind over matter, perhaps, but the fact remains that the recoil kick is physically the same in both cases. This is the difference between real and perceived recoil.

Recoil may be tamed a little if you can carry a heavier rifle (with lead or tungsten inserts in the rifle butt) and can afford a muzzle brake system. The latter is usually in the form of slits at the end of the rifle barrel. These are shaped to stop the muzzle from kicking upward and to lower the recoil; accuracy improves in any case. Note that the noise level increases a bit, so put plugs in your ears. Another way to lessen the effect of recoil is to make sure that the rifle butt (preferably with a thick rubber pad) is in intimate contact with your shoulder when you fire. A small gap is sufficient to transform the unpleasant impulse into a thump like a foundry hammer. If you are hunting big game, the chances are that you will be toting a rifle of at least calibre .375 H&H Magnum. This is my favourite calibre, since it fulfills all legal requirements, it has a good range, and the recoil is fairly acceptable, allowing the use of a telescopic sight. The big rifles, chambered in calibre .416 Rigby, the .458 and .460 magnums, and the .505 Gibbs, .600 and .700 Nitro Express are really the tools of the PH, since they are whopper stoppers, ideal for following up wounded animals. There is usually no telescopic sight on these shoulder shakers because scopes don't stand up well to the massive recoil, which smashes them up internally. If you want a longer, pain-free shooting career, select a rifle and bullet combination that you can handle accurately—and that means being able to bear the recoil.

Associated with recoil is a side effect that I've called "red eyebrow syndrome." No, I don't mean irritation. I mean red as in blood. Most rifles today, except for the very large calibre PH rifles, are equipped with a telescopic sight. This device is a great aid to precise bullet placement, and it can even double for binoculars in an emergency. A danger lies in the fact that when the hunter is aiming he concentrates on the target and, unconsciously, may bring his eye too near to the rear-end of the sight. The distance between the eye and the scope then becomes less than the recoil path. "Ah, ah," says the hunter, "this is a trophy animal," and he sets all in motion for the shot. The rifle spews forth its lead and recoils. The telescopic sight, being an integral part of the rifle, comes along for the ride. The ride stops right on the hunter's eyebrow. Payment is a semicircular wad cut out of your eyebrow worthy of a round with a heavyweight boxer. Ouch! You will need a good cuts man to stop the blood. Also, everybody looks at you, and you feel ashamed. Only nonexperienced hunters get "scoped," don't they? Now, would you mind passing me a plaster, please?

Eyes

Eye protection is often neglected, but a damaged eye may mean the end of your hunting days. Apart from self-inflicted damage such as scoping, the bush is full of dangers to your eyes. I would have had a bad experience with a Mozambique spitting cobra, as mentioned earlier, had I not been wearing my glasses. There's always a risk of a thorn's being driven deeply into your eyeball by a back-slashing branch when you are stalking. Definitely not recommended. Some caterpillars have brittle hairs on them that can easily get into your eyes and cause serious irritation and secondary infection. Protective glasses can prevent such accidents from happening or reduce the seriousness should they occur. Tinted shades can also reduce glare and improve contrast, which aids spotting and shooting. So, put something between your eyes and the rest of the world.

Safety with Weapons

With dangerous animals, it's the dead ones that get up and kill you. With guns and rifles it is unloaded weapons that suddenly go bang, issuing someone his ticket to heaven or hell. There are many tales about how the rifle was empty and on safety, but the accident still occurred. The following gives a few tips about avoiding the "safe" rifle syndrome.

Check the Barrel

It is elementary, but a rifle or shotgun barrel must be free of blockages to allow exit of the projectiles. If the exit is blocked, the pressure in the barrel can cause barrel distortion, or worse. Also, the accuracy of the currently fired bullet may be impaired, as well as that of future shots. A peek down the barrel, after having opened the shotgun or removing the firing bolt of the rifle, will take about two seconds. It could save you a lot more time otherwise spent looking for wounded animals, getting the weapon repaired or, worse still, recuperating in hospital. When a barrel explodes, it will deliver a swarm of shrapnel right into your face. It's amazing what you can find inside a rifle or shotgun barrel: Leaves, sticks, insects, pieces of cartridge, bits of cleaning rag, debris from bullets, and excessive oil are a few. A rifle barrel, in particular, should be as clean and as free of oil as possible before you set out for a hunt. An "oil shot" will be high because of reduced friction in the barrel; the bullet will not go where it should.

It is also elementary, but, after having checked that the barrel is free, make sure that you put the correct cartridge or shot shell into it. For instance, a 76-millimetre

12-gauge magnum long shot shell will also fit into a standard 12-gauge shotgun, chambered for a 70-millimetre shell. So what? I'll tell you what: If you squeeze the trigger you will get a big bang as the excess pressure explodes the barrel. Your face might also be rearranged in the process.

As a general rule: Load the weapon so that at no time the business end points at anything or anyone. Make sure that the barrel points only at the intended target. Accidents have occurred when a firing pin is inadvertently struck during loading. Never, ever trust the safety catch. The Fates, aided and abetted by the infamous Mr. Murphy, can get up to deadly mischief and turn a safety catch into an unreliable and willful piece of machinery with a mind of its own. Dangerous stuff, indeed.

Chapter 18

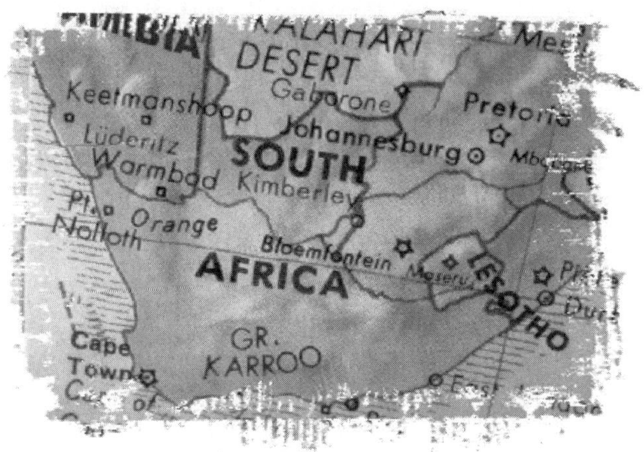

Hunt's End

The rifles and shotguns have been stripped down and cleaned. Their dry, cracked, and dented wooden butts and front shafts have been anointed and rubbed with oil and now shine like new. Even the inside of the barrels have been treated with a fluid that has dissolved the smearing of copper left by the passage of high-speed bullets. You know it's worked because the initially colourless liquid became bluish green, like verdigris on a bronze statue. Your fingers, over the weeks of safari, had rubbed the bluing from parts of the rifle barrel and had caused silvery blemishes on it. You have therefore rubbed down the affected areas, degreased them, and applied yet another fluid. The wonders of chemistry have made those areas dark blue again. You make a mental note that you will avoid holding the barrel there, in future. You know—just what you said to yourself last time. Old habits die hard.

You take each weapon in your hands and place it into its designated slot in the gun safe. Wearing their fresh coats of oil, they gleam at you like sleek, wet seals. When all the weapons have been replaced, you close the door on the safe and spin the combination lock. The rattling clicks of the device remind you of the clicking of the warthog's tusks. Or was it the honey badger's teeth? No matter, it is the end of the hunt, for a while. You check the boxes of cartridges, noting that you will have to order more for the next hunt. You rearrange the remaining few bullets in their boxes. They now sit next to each other; death, waiting in orderly rows. It is now a good time to reflect on hunting.

Hunting is an activity that must be acknowledged at all levels of society to be acceptable. It will be politically acceptable if it is shown to be humane and ecologically sustainable and if it makes economic sense and succeeds in creating an environment in which humans and animals can live together. For farmers that means reduced losses from crop damage and livestock predation. For others it means safety from attack by wild animals. Animal control must not cost the taxpayer anything, because such things are unpopular, from the start, with Joe Public. Hunting, then, must be recognized by society to be a service for environmental protection, a provider of jobs, and a cheap, effective, and humanely applied instrument for maintaining healthy and balanced animal populations. Hunting must be seen by all to be the intelligent use of a renewable resource; only then is it going to be morally acceptable. It is the duty of every hunter to strive to meet these requirements, in all aspects.

If the above conditions are viewed in the light of what the attitude to hunting was, say, only thirty years ago, it's obvious that we have a whole new ballgame. The world has changed, and with it the rules of hunting. Formerly vast areas of suitable habitat for many species have been lost because of human usurpation of space. Forests have been cleared, marshes drained, and valleys filled with water. Our generally negative impact on the land and water has been considerable during the last hundred years. None of this concerned governments or people at the beginning of the present century. But as the year 2000 begins to peep coyly over the horizon, and the human race reaches out boldly for even more land, we must start the search for new and better solutions. It's not going to be an easy task.

The old celebrity trophy hunters like Hemingway and Ruark are no more. They experienced and wrote about African hunting as it was in the past. The idea of conservation or of game animals having to pay their way were unknown to them. There were millions of hectares of unspoiled wilderness then, all teeming with animals, and the exploitation of these resources by man was definitely a one-sided affair. This fact is clearly reflected in the way Hemingway and Ruark describe their hunts. The world has changed a lot since then. Game farming, management, marketing, and modern conservation have created new rules whereby strict, professional selection of old and biologically exhausted (nonbreeding) trophy animals allows the sustainable use of renewable resources.

Trophy fees for today's hunts are very high, but the hard currency injection ensures the existence of the environment and the species in it. This is an essential source of revenue for poor African countries. The principles of "if it pays, it stays" and "use it or lose it" now prevail everywhere in modern conservation and hunting strategies.

Trophy hunting today should not aim to worship at the holy grail of record-book entries, but to act as a service for game management. Sure, most old animals will be bearing enough horn, tusk, or skull length to obtain permanent fame in the book and, if you get lucky, well then, go ahead and get your trophy registered. If your trophy falls short by some fraction of an inch below trophy size, then that's too bad, but, it is *how* you have obtained it that counts. It is whether the animal was the right one that matters.

Another aspect about trophy hunting is the secondary jobs that it creates. A hunter employs his PH, the trackers, skinners, cooks, and camp personnel. He pays them with hard currency. After the hunt, another group of native labourers is employed with the preparation of the trophies. This branch of the business encourages the learning of skills, educates the personnel in biology, and provides gainful employment to those who, having a family to feed but no income, might be tempted to poach. After the trophies have been prepared, they have to be exported. The government office responsible for this controls the licenses and the legality of the trophies. The issuing of export documents employs others who are paid for via license fees and taxes. The hunter again pays all of this. When the trophies are given clearance, they are freighted and exported. People are employed here, as well. Freighting and airport cargo costs are all paid for by the hunter, which means the hunter pays their wages—yet another injection to the economy of the exporting land. That's it. Hard facts to swallow for idealists. The value added to even a small, common steenbok, for example, is phenomenal. Take the case of a hunter who wants a record-book steenbok. Ignoring the initial travel costs, the PH's daily fee will be around $400 US. A minimum of seven days for a plains game hunt is usually booked. The trophy fee will be around $300 US, and the record-book entry fee about $10 US. The trophy preparation, as a shoulder mount, will cost about $300 US, and the freighting and sundry costs another $300 US. Even estimated conservatively, the death of one small and common animal will bring nearly $4,000 US to the host land. Big bucks, indeed, for a small buck.

With new game-management methods—in particular, those involving the local population and making them aware that they have a common resource—game animals are not regarded as a nuisance anymore. Communities have become aware of the value of a well-maintained game population. The hard currency brought in by trophy hunters is encouragement enough for the people to protect their renewable resources. No one wants to kill the geese that continue to lay golden eggs. Also, game can exist on marginal land that is of no use for crops, and the meat from trophy hunting provides a cheap source of high-value protein to the local population.

Our ancestors hunted for meat, and they also obtained other useful animal products, such as horns and antlers for tools and skins for clothing. No ecological constraints existed, so modern selection criteria were not applied. Also, there were more places for animals to live, since there were fewer humans around. The modern hunter faces a different situation, one now requiring careful management of habitat and species. Will coming generations hunt? I believe that they will. I believe that they must, and that their prime task will be to ensure the survival of game species by means of environmental protection. So, if you think about it carefully, hunting now and in the future has really nothing to do anymore with trophy size, expressions of gender-related superiority, or other such nonsense. Hunting has assumed a profound significance. Hunting is about the survival of the hunted species. And survival, like hunting, is an instinct that persists.